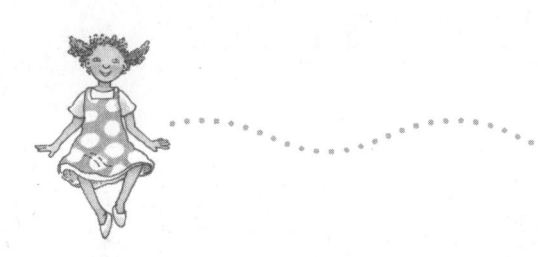

Jump, Wiggle, Twirl & Giggle!

25 Fun and Easy Movement Activities for Every Day

by Roberta Altman

SCHOLASTIC
PROFESSIONAL BOOKS

New York • Toronto • London • Auckland • Sydney
Mexico City • New Delhi • Hong Kong

There are many people to thank for helping make my dream of writing this book come true. At Scholastic Professional Books, Terry Cooper and Deborah Schecter for their patience and helpfulness; at Bank Street College, Ellen Schecter and Elisabeth Jakab for making it all possible; at home, my husband, Neil, and children, Lisa and Amanda, for their support. Thanks also to Becca Kessler, who first told me the beautiful Hawaiian folktale about the snails. Also to my colleague Nina Jaffe, many thanks for sharing her knowledge and expertise on drumming for the Ghanaian Talking Drum lesson. I am very grateful to Ann-Marie Mott of the Bank Street School for Children for her wonderful photographs. Finally, all my thanks and appreciation to the many children, teachers, and teachers-in-training who have inspired my work over the years.

"Dream Variation" from COLLECTED POEMS by Langston Hughes. Copyright © 1994 by the Estate of Langston Hughes. Reprinted by permission of Alfred A. Knopf, a division of Random House, Inc.

Scholastic Inc. grants teachers permission to photocopy the story on page 43 for classroom use. No other part of this publication may be reproduced in whole or in part, or stored in a retrieval system, or transmitted in any form or by any means, electronic, mechanical, photocopying, recording, or otherwise, without written permission of the publisher. For information regarding permission, write to Scholastic Inc., 555 Broadway, New York, NY 10012.

Cover design by Jaime Lucero

Cover artwork by Nadine Bernard Westcott

Interior design by Sydney Wright

Interior photographs by Ann-Marie Mott

Interior artwork by James Graham Hale

ISBN: 0-590-01972-4
Copyright © 2000 The Bank Street College of Education.

All rights reserved.
Printed in the U.S.A.

Contents

INTRODUCTION
How Movement Empowers a Child's Development and Learning 4
An Overview of the Movement Activities 5
Sample Movement Menus 7
Helpful Tips for Integrating Movement Into Your Daily and Yearlong Program 8
Planning a Movement Program 10
Comprehensive Assessment Checklist 13

GETTING STARTED
  Warm-Up 14
  Aerobics 18
  Cool-Down 21
  Refresher Quickies 24
  Transition Tidbits 26
  Relaxations 29

LANGUAGE ARTS
  Inside/Outside ★ Naming Your Place in Space 33
  Toys That Move ★ Using Action Words 36
  A Snail's Story ★ Folktales Come Alive 40
  Whirl, Whirl! ★ Poetry in Motion 45
  Obstacle Course Search ★ Finding the Words 50

SOCIAL STUDIES
  The Circus ★ People Who Work With Animals 54
  The Ghanaian Talking Drum ★ Sounds From Another Culture 58
  Pack Up the Produce! ★ Where Our Food Comes From 61
  Become a Machine ★ Learning How Things Work 65
  Dragon Dance ★ Celebrating Chinese New Year 70

MATH
  Jumping Numbers ★ Using Counting and Sequencing 76
  Bodies in Motion ★ Learning About Shapes 80
  Design a Dance ★ Inventing Patterns 84
  Parachute Games ★ Exploring One-to-One Correspondence 87

SCIENCE
  Falling Leaves ★ Exploring Seasonal Changes 92
  Snowflakes and Icicles ★ Freezing and Thawing 95
  Monkey Make-Believe ★ Life in a Rainforest 99
  Balancing Buildings ★ Discovering Gravity 103
  A Spaghetti Feast ★ Changes in Properties 108

Introduction

How Movement Empowers a Child's Development and Learning

Children learn about themselves and their world through physical exploration, discovery, and interaction with their surroundings, using what Howard Gardner called kinesthetic intelligence. At this stage of life, they are "wired" for cognitive, social, and emotional learning through their bodies. Piaget called this the sensory-motor stage of development, the hallmark of the way young children learn. As teachers, you see the evidence everywhere as children squirm and settle in meetings, shift about during class, or bound away to play. Physicality also plays a key role in a child's school life. As their teacher, you can help children develop their full mental and physical potential by harnessing this kinesthetic intelligence through the use of some or all of the movement activities outlined in this book.

Guided movement gives children a way to explore rhythm, space, their imagination, and the physical makeup and capacities of their own bodies. It also helps them develop self-awareness, cooperation, and a sense of belonging to and contributing to the group. Sharing space, ideas, and movement creations helps children bond with the group and build a sense of community. Movement empowers the cognitive dimension of learning as well: Carrying out an activity requires concentrating, following directions, problem solving, using language in new contexts, generating original ideas, and finding ways to communicate them. The psychological benefits include the satisfaction of experiencing the mind and body working together in a creative process, cooperating socially, and, possibly, interacting cross-culturally.

An Overview of the Movement Activities

The movement activities in this book will help you nurture and direct children's energy and learning potential with step-by-step programs that support your management strategies. The activities will help create a cooperative atmosphere in the classroom, and increase children's self-awareness and skills in physical expression and self-control. The activities are easy to do, and most require no special equipment. They can be done inside the average classroom, are connected to the curriculum, and can help channel your students' energies constructively.

Here's an overview of how each lesson is constructed:

Description and Learning Goals: Each lesson is briefly described, including the specific skills children will learn.

Materials: Often, all that is needed is taped music or a drum. Any other materials that may be required are usually available in the average classroom. However, there are suggestions for expanding the lesson that may call for unusual materials and three activities are specifically geared for special equipment.

Warm-Up: To help you motivate students and stimulate discussion and ideas, this section provides you with general background information and preparatory activities related to the lesson theme.

Creative Movement: This section is presented in a step-by-step format to help you easily organize and manage the activities. Examples of language to use and the kind of responses you can expect from children are also included.

Extending the Lesson: Suggestions are presented for additional activities and/or other areas to explore.

Assessment Checklist: Key learning skills are identified, with suggestions for what to watch for in each activity.

Resources: This section provides a list of books, music, and other supporting materials.

Sample Movement Menus

A Complete Movement Class (40 minutes)
1. Begin with the Warm-Up activity—5 minutes
2. Continue with the Aerobics activity—5 minutes
3. Choose from thematic movement activities in language arts, social studies, math, or science—25 minutes
4. End with the Cool-Down activity—5 minutes

Classroom Activity (5–10 minutes)
1. Circle Time: Refresher Quickies—5 minutes
2. Ending the Day: Relaxations—5 minutes

Curriculum Connections (30 minutes)
1. Begin with the Warm-Up activity—5 minutes
2. Choose from thematic movement activities in language arts, social studies, math or science—20 minutes
3. End with the Cool-Down activity—5 minutes

Helpful Tips for Integrating Movement Into Your Daily and Yearlong Program

Location

Movement can be done anytime and just about anywhere. The most comfortable place to start is probably your own classroom. Establish certain spaces in the room as the movement areas. Have a meeting with children and clearly indicate the borders of each space, where to wait, where to move, and where to end the lesson. If it is feasible, you might want to use masking tape on the floor to outline the areas you will use.

Here are some ideas about how you can use specific classroom spaces:

- The meeting area serves well for Warm-Up, Relaxations, partner activities, and some curriculum-linked lessons, especially in language arts.

- Table or desk areas can be cleared by students and teachers by pushing the furniture to a designated spot along the edges of the room. A wide-open space lends itself to longer movement sessions, aerobic activities, and the use of equipment. Establish clear routines for who will move the furniture and how.

- The block area can be cleared on specified days so that it can be used for movement activities.

Other usable spaces in the school include hallways, the cafeteria, the auditorium stage, the gym, or outdoor areas such as the playground or practice fields. Apply the routines you have established for designating the use of space in your classroom to any such area.

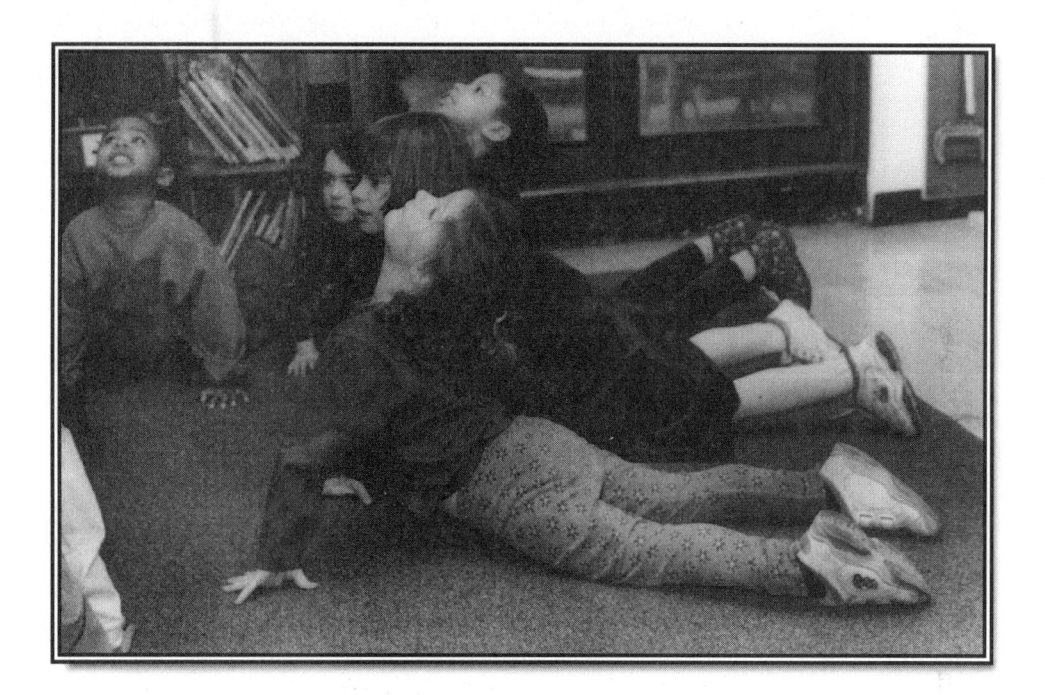

Duration and Scheduling

Movement sessions can last anywhere from 5 to 40 minutes, depending on your purposes (check the Sample Movement Menus, page 7). They can also be used throughout the school day and year. It is a good idea to balance scheduled movement lessons with spontaneous ones—occasions when you think some physical activity will enhance the day. These can include such activities as Relaxations following outdoor time and creative interpretations after watching a snowfall.

You may want to make movement sessions part of your daily routine. For instance, a partner-game session can enhance the meeting time by setting a cooperative tone, or warm-up exercises can get students' minds and bodies working together. You can also use movement sessions to manage transitions; for example, prepare children for rest or quiet time by making calming exercises a familiar part of the routine. Other ways to use movement activities follow.

Integrate movement into the curriculum: Any subject you teach can be expanded and enlivened with a movement component. You can also plan a movement activity to follow special excursions, such as a trip to the park to study snails or to gather fall leaves.

Include movement in school community events: Movement helps bring people together and builds a sense of community. Put on a circus and invite younger groups to watch (see The Circus, page 54); act out a favorite story for parents (see A Snail's Story, page 40); contribute to a school assembly with a performance of poetry in motion (see Whirl, Whirl!, page 45); or have an intergenerational classroom picnic, with everyone participating in parachute games (see Parachute Games, page 87).

Planning a Movement Program

Like any other subject, movement works best if you establish regular routines with clear guidelines. When children know what to expect and how to use their bodies properly, they have better self-control and are better equipped to enjoy lively activity.

The essential ingredients of a successful program include:

The Movement Routine

1. Start each session with a brief reminder about the space to be used and the No Bumping rule.

2. Make a "What We Do in Movement" poster that includes: Warm-Up, Aerobics, Thematic Activity, and Cool-Down.

3. Talk to children about the theme for the day, and remind them of the order of activities.

Developing Themes

This book suggests some curriculum themes suitable for early childhood. You can also adapt any theme by identifying its essential components and matching them with the elements of movement. For example, during a math lesson using Unifix cubes, children learn that color patterns have a sequence that repeats. Children expand and reinforce learning when they make up a variety of motions (hop, spin, wiggle), put them in a sequence and repeat them. Each theme lesson provides a model for matching subject components with movement elements. Consider putting together a planning sheet to integrate movement with other subjects and/or themes.

Assessment

Physical learning, the kinesthetic intelligence described by Howard Gardner, utilizes many of a child's capacities: observation, imitation, coordination, and interpretation. Movement activities develop an essential connection between mind and body.

To help you analyze a child's learning style and ability during movement activities, I've listed the elements of a possible Comprehensive Assessment Checklist on the next page. You may want to use all or parts of this checklist throughout the year to assess each child's progress and to identify areas of strength and weakness.

Comprehensive Assessment Checklist

Social Skills
* cooperates with others
* can work alone or as a group member
* can initiate ideas or respond to those of other children
* respects personal and shared space; is aware of self and others

Emotional Skills
* perseveres when working on a problem or skill
* enthusiastically participates and engages
* can stay focused and involved in the lesson
* can engage in the give-and-take of group activities

Cognitive Abilities/Capacities
* can orient him- or herself in space: in the center, edges, front, and back, and on high, medium, and low levels
* can observe and imitate demonstrated movements
* can remember, practice, and repeat a sequence of movements or steps

Physical Skills/Abilities
* has basic locomotor skills: can run, hop, spin, skip, gallop, leap
* knows how to find and maintain his or her balance
* has developed coordination, agility, flexibility; can carry out movements quickly and accurately

Creativity and Rhythmic Abilities
* can invent motions or gestures to convey an idea or feeling
* can carry out and repeat a sequence of invented steps to create his or her own dance
* takes risks or tries new ways of doing things
* can find and stay on the beat or with the rhythm
* responds to changes in tempo or mood of music

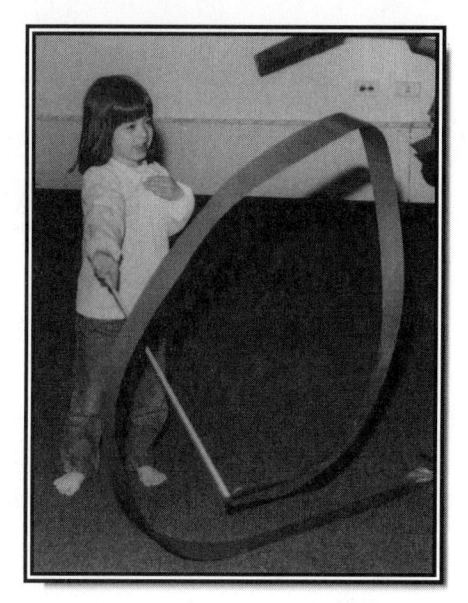

GETTING STARTED

Warm-Up

These stretching and strengthening exercises prepare students for the more vigorous activities to come. Doing them to a beat helps coordination and creates an energizing atmosphere.

Materials

- taped music or a drum

Warm-Up

Choose a spot in the room where children can stretch out both arms without bumping someone else. Tell them this will be their personal space for the exercises. Then explain that the stretches and strengthening exercises they are going to do will give their bodies better tone and help prevent injuries. Stress that all physical activities—whether creative movement, jogging, or sports—need to start with a warm-up, and they should get in the habit of doing such exercises before any activity.

GETTING STARTED

Creative Movement

1 Arm Stretches: Have children stand in their personal space with their feet about 1-1/2 feet apart. Ask them to reach first the right arm, then the left arm, straight up so they can feel a good pull down each side of the body. Repeat four times.

Next, have children stretch out their arms sideways. Then, with their knees slightly bent (to prevent injury), have them tilt way over to the right side until the right hand touches the right foot. Repeat on the left side.

Finally, ask children to make full, reaching arm circles using one arm at a time, four times for each arm.

2 Leg Power: Count out loud as children do 10 Jumping Jacks (an exercise in which arms and legs are coordinated by opening and closing at the same time).

Test children's strength and balance by having them focus their eyes on a particular spot and, with their arms extended to the side, slowly lifting up one foot until the thigh is parallel to the ground. Then have them hold that position without falling or hopping while counting to four.

3 Body Stretch: Ask children to sit on the floor with the soles of their feet together and their hands holding on to their ankles. Have them gently bounce their knees up and down, then slowly pull their heads toward their feet. Repeat four times.

GETTING STARTED

Next, tell them to spread their legs out wide, lean forward, and bounce gently. Repeat four times. Finally, have them straighten their legs to the front. Then ask them to imagine their legs are like a tightrope and their fingers are the acrobats, and have them walk the fingers of both hands from the top of the thighs to their toes and back. Repeat four times.

4 **Mind and Body Ready:** Conclude the warm-up by asking children to close their eyes, breathe in through the nose and slowly blow a small stream of air out through the mouth. Ask them to repeat this three times, then ask them to open their eyes, fold up their legs, and get ready for Aerobics (see page 18).

GETTING STARTED

Resources

MUSIC
Everybody Dance (Cassette or CD). Chime Time: 1-800-477-5075.

Extending the Lesson

Many children have family members who warm up before jogging or taking classes in dance, martial arts, or yoga. Invite a parent or relative to lead the class in one of his or her warm-up exercises. Let students cut out magazine pictures of people exercising and glue them onto a mural collage.

Assessment Checklist

In order to learn movement, children must develop the capacity to "see and do"—to copy motions the teacher demonstrates. Here's what to watch for:

* Can students accurately replicate the movements?
* Do children know where to put arms, legs, and head?
* Are children flexible and limber enough to do the leg stretches?
* Can students relax and calm themselves as well as exercise?

GETTING STARTED

Aerobics

Vigorous exercise is essential for building muscular and cardiovascular strength. Children should learn the importance of developing lifelong habits of exercise. This activity also gives children practice controlling their bodies in space and in relation to others.

Materials

- taped music or a drum
- colored plastic hoops (see Resources, page 20) or colored construction paper cut into circles, squares, triangles, stars, and rectangles (tape together several large sheets)

Warm-Up

Designate the space to be used during the activities. Tell children there are only two rules: First, have fun! Second, do not bump into anyone or anything. Explain the idea of aerobics: that moving fast makes your heart and lungs work harder to bring oxygen to fuel the muscles that let you run and jump. Your heart is a muscle, too, and it needs this exercise to stay strong and healthy. Ask children to help

GETTING STARTED

generate some tips or rules for moving as quickly as possible without losing control, bumping into things, or falling down. You may want to chart these ideas and post them.

Creative Movement

1 Place hoops or construction paper shapes on the floor in the designated movement space (about one object for every two children). Then ask one or two children to demonstrate running, skipping, or hopping around the room in one direction. Now announce that when you begin the music or drumbeat, all children should do the same. But when the music or drum stops, they must freeze and then tiptoe to a hoop or shape. Tell them they are learning self-control and the object is to stop right away and then move into close quarters on a hoop or shape without bumping each other.

2 Add variety by suggesting several gaits, such as galloping, skipping, hopping, jumping, running, and so on. While children are moving, take away one or two hoops or shapes. Then stop the music and remind children to enter and share the more crowded space gently, using their "hugging arms." Continue the game until you have five or six children to a hoop or shape.

GETTING STARTED

Resources

MUSIC
Drums of Passion
Baba Olatunji.
Columbia.

EQUIPMENT
Colored plastic hoops.
Chime Time:
1-800-477-5075
www.chimetime.com

Extending the Lesson

Help children sharpen listening skills and add to the fun by selecting a different instrument to play for each gait; for example, play a triangle for tiptoeing, jingle bells for hopping, sticks for galloping, and so on. To help children remember the cues for each instrument and gait, make a chart and post it.

Assessment Checklist

Children can connect mind and body more closely with the help of sound cues. It is also very important to the development of young children to master the basic movement gaits. Look for:

* the way each student handles the basic movements of running, galloping, hopping, spinning, stomping, tiptoeing, as well as starting and stopping, in response to rhythmic cues

* the speed of each student's reflexes in responding to sound cues

GETTING STARTED

Cool-Down

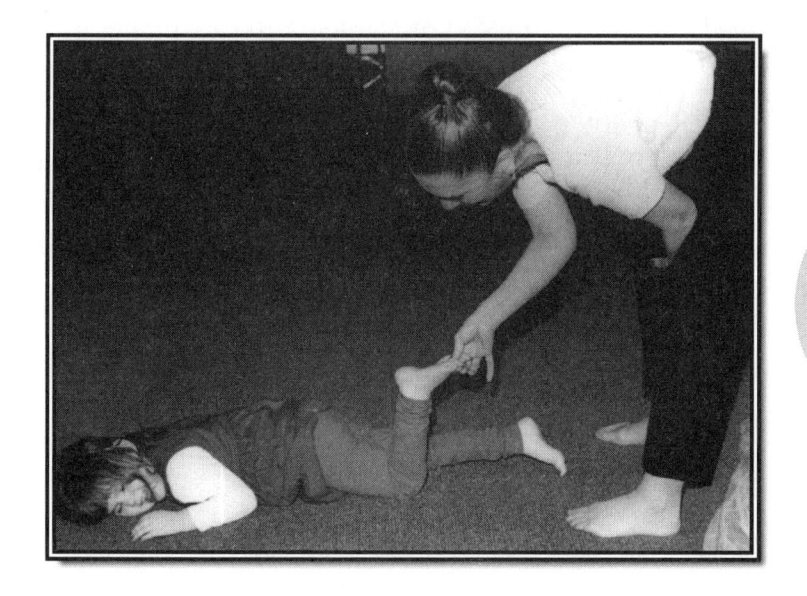

Children learn and experience how mind and body can work together to relax and refresh muscles after lively exercise.

Materials

* soothing music on tape, a small bell, or a triangle

Warm-Up

Ask children how they can tell that they've gotten a good workout. (a rapid heartbeat, rapid breathing, sweating) Tell them these are all positive signs, evidence that they have been exercising hard enough to build up their strength.

Then tell them that they need to practice relaxing just as much as any other exercise. Relaxation helps the muscles go back to their regular positions and the heart slow down to a normal rate. Once children learn how to do this, they will be able to begin their next activity refreshed and ready to go.

GETTING STARTED

Creative Movement

1 Have children lie down on their backs on the floor. Tell them they will be using their brains to send a resting message to each part of the body you indicate. The idea is to rest the parts of the body one by one, until every part from toes to head is limp.

2 Put on soothing music (or use the triangle or bell). Ask children to close their eyes, listen to your voice and the music, and breathe in slowly through the nose and out through the mouth (repeat three times). Tell them to send a resting message to their toes and feet first. Then continue progressively up the body: "Rest your lower and upper legs, calf muscles, and thigh muscles. Rest your stomach and back. Rest your chest. Rest your shoulders. Relax your neck and the muscles in your face. Breathe in through the nose and out through the mouth. Keep breathing as you listen to the music and let your brain rest, too." Take your time with the relaxation messages to give children a chance to "hear and do." The entire activity can take three to five minutes.

3 As you come to the end of the exercise, explain to children that they need to get up slowly and quietly. Say you will give each child a tap when it is his or her turn to slowly get up and walk softly or tiptoe to the door, their desks, the meeting circle (or wherever you want them to go next) without waking up anyone else. Give them a final challenge: "Let's see who can do this without making a single sound."

GETTING STARTED

Resources

BOOKS
Yoga for Children by Mary Stewart and Kathy Phillips. Simon & Schuster, 1992.

Yoga for Children by Stella Weller. Thomsons, 1996.

MUSIC
The Fairie Round Shelley Phillips and Friends. Gourd Music, P.O. Box 585, Felton, CA 95018.

4 End with children calm and ready to transition smoothly to the next activity. Draw on these exercises throughout the day whenever children need a change of pace or to get focused and steady again. (See Relaxations, page 29.)

Extending the Lesson

To increase children's awareness of themselves and each other, have them do the full body relaxations with a partner. First, one does the relaxation exercises, then the partner checks to see if she or he is truly relaxed by using the "rag doll" test—taking a hand or foot and gently shaking it to make sure it is loose. Ask children to share ways they relax at home, and try out some of those ideas too.

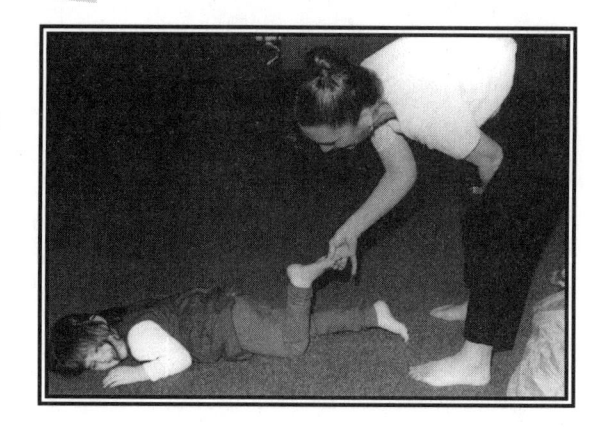

Talk with students about different exercise methods for relaxing the body. Show them books on yoga and tai chi and have them try some of the movements. Tell them that many positions in these exercise systems are based on animal movements. If their parents or friends take such classes, ask if they will come and share an exercise session with children.

Assessment Checklist

These exercises leave children rested yet alert in mind and body. Here are some things to look for:

* How does a child respond to the rag doll test?
* Can students listen to verbal cues and carry out the physical activity?

GETTING STARTED

Refresher Quickies

These simple exercises energize both the muscles and the mind, thereby helping children continue their activities in a refreshed and alert way. The exercises can also be used to teach children the names of body parts and how muscles and bones work together.

Materials

- taped music or a drum

Warm-Up

Talk to children about learning to exercise while staying in one spot. Ask them to think about how each part of the body has its own way of moving. Discuss those joints—such as the ball-and-socket joints of the shoulders and hips—that allow circular movements. Point out that wrists and ankles have similar joints, made up of many small bones that allow for full rotation.

Creative Movement

Do head and shoulder circles and have children repeat your motions. Ask volunteers to show circling motions with other body parts, such as ankles, wrists, torso, and arms. Repeat each motion four times. Then put them together in a sequence: head, shoulders, arms, wrists, ankles, knees, torso.

GETTING STARTED

Resources

BOOKS
The Children's Atlas of the Human Body by Richard Walker. The Millbrook Press, 1994.

The Children's Book of the Body. Copper Beech Books, 1996.

Outside-in by Clare Smallman. Barron's, 1986.

MUSIC
Movin'. Hap Palmer. Educational Activities, Inc. Freeport, NY

2 Ask children to look for similarities and differences in the ways various parts of the body can make circles. For instance, because the shoulders and hips both have ball-and-socket joints, arms and legs can make full, wide circles. However, since the elbow is a hinge joint, it can only move fully in two directions. Chart other student responses, ask for demonstrations, and add them to your repertoire of motions.

3 Conclude the lesson and create a calm atmosphere by asking children to make the body-part circles in slow motion. Play slow, soothing music (or tap softly on the drum) to accompany this portion of the lesson.

Extending the Lesson

Throughout the year, continue to explore all the ways these body parts can move. Tape up a Movement Recipe chart that names a body part in one column and the motion to make with it in another. For variation, children can try doing the movements as wiggles or shakes as well as making circles fast or slow. Or try having children choose a different motion for each body part.

Assessment Checklist

This lesson engages children in learning about body parts, varieties of motion, and range of motion (the full extent to which each part can move). Students develop a valuable foundation in both vocabulary and movement. Things to notice are whether:

* Children can identify each body part by name and location
* Children accurately match verbal cues with physical motions
* Children can contribute new ideas for combinations of movements

GETTING STARTED

Transition Tidbits

Throughout the school day, children move from one area or activity to another. Add some order and fun to these transitions by teaching children to become more aware of each other and to focus on where they are going.

Materials

- taped music, drum, or jingle bells
- masking tape (optional)

Warm-Up

Choose one of the following two "tidbits" that best suits your needs, "mirroring" or "wiggle walks." If, for example, you are lining up children in pairs to go to lunch or outdoor play, mirroring is probably your best choice. If children are waiting to go somewhere one by one, such as the bathroom or to get book bags and coats, then try wiggle walks.

Creative Movement: Mirroring

Tell children to choose a partner by turning to face the person nearest them. Ask them to decide who is to be the leader and who the follower (they will switch later on).

GETTING STARTED

2. Tell children that the leaders are going to start by putting the palms of their hands together and making slow, smooth motions (making circles, raising and lowering their hands, moving their hands from side to side like windshield wipers, and so on). The follower is to imitate these movements. Before everyone starts, ask pairs of volunteers to demonstrate their motions in front of the class.

3. Add variety to the exercise by asking partners to match different body parts—touching nose to nose, elbow to elbow, foot to foot, and so on. Now put on slow, flowing music (or use the drum or bells) and instruct children to begin their mirroring motions. Tell them you will call on a pair at a time to stand up and match walking steps as they get on line to go to lunch, the playground, on a trip, or anywhere. Then ask children to switch leader and follower roles and repeat the exercise.

Extending the Lesson

Here's how to add an element of surprise: Make 10 to 15 drawings of body parts on separate pieces of paper. Fold them up and put them in a paper bag. Then ask a child to pull one out, open it, and announce the body part the partners will mirror next. If, for instance, the child takes out a picture of a foot, the partners will touch foot to foot.

Creative Movement: Wiggle Walk

1. Designate the pathway for the wiggle walk (from the meeting area to cubbies, for instance). If feasible, use masking tape to mark the route. Tell children that one way to vary their wiggle walk is to do it on tiptoe or in slow motion, with very fast long steps, or with very short, quick steps. Ask them to think of other ways.

Suggest that they also do the wiggle walk on different levels:
* stretch and reach arms to the ceiling while walking on the balls of the feet;
* try a stomping walk on the middle level (hunched over);
* squat and walk like a duck on the low level.

27

GETTING STARTED

Resources

BOOKS
How Does the Wind Walk? by Nancy White Carlstrom. Simon & Schuster, 1993.

Mirror Magic by Seymour Simon. Boyds Mills Press, 1991.

Mirrors: Finding Out About the Properties of Light by Bernie Zubrowski. William Morrow, 1992.

Walk With Me by Naomi Davis. Cartwheel, 1995.

MUSIC
One World. Putumayo World Music. Various artists.

Extending the Lesson

Introduce children to the concept of qualities—for example, smooth, wiggly, sharp, or soft. Suggest that they incorporate two or more of these qualities into a walk—for instance, tiptoeing while wiggling. Children can have a hilarious time thinking up wacky combinations, such as squatting and walking like a duck going backward.

Assessment Checklist

Both the mirroring and wiggle walk activities require cooperation and concentration. This game gives children good practice in learning to read movements ("see and do"). The ability to replicate demonstrations is important for learning other skills, such as handwriting. Here are some things to notice:

✸ Can children follow the motions of their partner?

✸ Can they handle the roles of both leader and follower?

✸ Do students create a variety of ways to walk?

GETTING STARTED

Relaxations

These simple breathing and stretching exercises enable children to calm and relax their bodies and thereby help their day go better.

Materials

* soothing taped music or triangle

Warm-Up

Help children learn to "read" their bodies by asking them to feel the difference between making tight fists and then relaxing them so that their palms, wrists, and fingers go limp. Ask them to describe this contrast and any strategies they used to make their muscles relax. Try this same exercise with a few other body parts, such as the stomach, arms, and legs. Discuss why it is a good idea to learn how to relax, and explain that their minds and bodies will work better if they make time to calm them. Then ask children to think about when to use relaxation procedures. Point out times during the school day when it is important to calm down and focus again (usually after play, toward the end of the day, or during transitions). Chart the ideas for future use.

GETTING STARTED

Creative Movement: Flickering Candle

1. Ask children to place their hands on their laps or their desks. Put on soothing music or play the triangle, and have them close their eyes, breathe in through the nose, and then blow a soft stream of air out through the mouth (repeat three times).

2. Tell children that they are now going to learn the technique of "blowing out the candle." Have them open their eyes and hold up their index fingers in front of their mouths. This finger will be their candle. Pantomime lighting the candle, and ask children to repeat the breathing exercise, this time blowing the soft stream of air onto the tip of their index fingers. Encourage them to imagine that the blown air makes a flame flicker but not go out. Repeat three times. (Note: This technique is especially useful for refocusing and calming children. It can be used anytime, anywhere.)

Creative Movement: Animal Stretches

1. Animal movements fascinate children. They will eagerly imitate the stretching, creeping, or slithering of any animal you suggest. Discuss how animals need to stretch and relax too. Ask for a few volunteers to show their favorite animal stretches. They may mimic a cat stretching or arching its back or a bird spreading out its wings. Talk about how stretching helps loosen up and thereby relax muscles.

GETTING STARTED

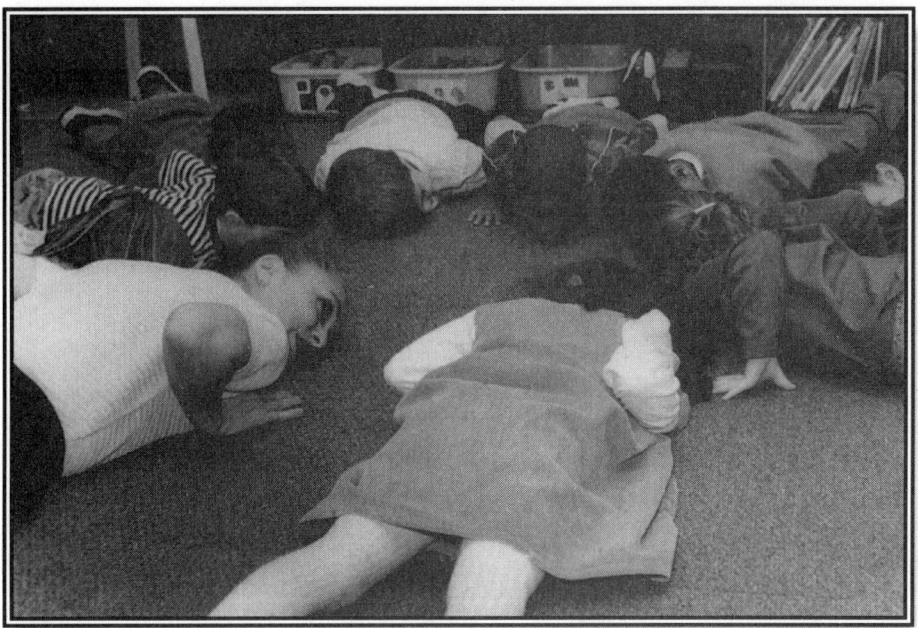

2 Ask children to arrange themselves in the meeting area or on the floor so they have enough personal space that they aren't touching someone else. Tell them to do the movements you are going to describe slowly and smoothly so that their muscles can stretch and then relax like a rubber band. (Take a rubber band and demonstrate what you mean by slowly stretching and then releasing it.)

3 Put on soothing music (or tap the triangle) and have children lie facedown on the floor, with their hands facing palms down under their shoulders. Tell them they will be doing a snake stretch. Then ask them to raise their heads and chests by pressing their hands down as you count to three.

4 Now ask them to pretend they are snakes, halfway out of their holes, that want to look around. While still up on their hands, ask children to twist their heads to the left as far back as possible to see what's behind them. Then have them do this on the right side. Repeat the left and right looks three times.

5 Ask the snakes to tip their heads straight back and look up. Repeat three times.

GETTING STARTED

Resources

BOOKS
A Yoga Parade of Animals by Pauline Mainland. Element Children's Books, 1998.

MUSIC
Clare de Lune. Claude Debussy.

6 Now that the snakes are finished looking around, have them slowly lower themselves back down and roll up into a ball. The snakes can "sleep" rolled up like this to the count of 10. (This is a very effective exercise for increasing flexibility in the spine and smoothing out tension in the back.)

Extending the Lesson

Use relaxation exercises during the day whenever they can help make things go more smoothly. For instance, at rest time put on soothing music and talk children through the full body relaxation exercise as soon as they lie down. Use Blowing out the Candle if you sense children getting frenetic.

Assessment Checklist

Children should learn to become aware of when they are feeling tense as well as how to make themselves relax. But to consciously do this takes considerable focus. Here are some things to notice:

* To what extent can children carry out your relaxation instructions?
* Can children recognize when they feel tense and then use their relaxation skills?

Language Arts

Inside/Outside
Naming Your Place in Space

This game helps children orient themselves in space by "naming the place." It also helps them build vocabulary: When children learn a word in connection with a direct action, it becomes cemented in their minds.

Materials

- lively taped music or drum
- colored plastic hoops (see Resources, page 20), colored construction paper cut into squares, circles, triangles, and so on (tape together several large sheets), or rug squares

Warm-Up

Ask children about all the places in a room where they can run, jump, and freeze. From contributions such as "*along* the edges," "*around* the middle," and "*in front* of the windows," make a chart of "place in space" words. Challenge students to add more phrases in other lessons, or leave the chart posted so they can add ideas as they think of them. Bring the chart to the next movement lesson to try some of them out. Phrases can become building blocks for movement sentences like *Jump in front of the windows; Run along the wall; Hop past the door.* These word exercises generate spatial awareness and help keep the activity organized and focused.

LANGUAGE ARTS

Creative Movement

1 Designate the activity area and "map" it out for children by walking through it. Explain that they can run along the edges of the area, but when the music stops, they must freeze in a hoop or on a shape or rug square in the center, or *inside*, of the room. Or tell them they can hop around the center and then tiptoe to the *outside* corners and freeze in or on a shape when they hear the drum stop. The challenge of listening for sound cues and finding the right place in space keeps children thinking and moving at the same time, creating a strong mind and body connection.

2 As children watch, lay out the place spaces by putting different-colored hoops, construction paper shapes, or rug squares on the inside, or center, of the room and some on the outside, in the corners. Explain to children that they will be running, skipping, or galloping to music (or drumbeats). When the music stops, children "put on the brakes" and freeze in a shape until you tell them to walk or tiptoe to the inside or outside hoops or shapes. Begin with instructions such as "Skip along the edges but listen for the music soon." Then give a little warning: "Okay, start listening for the music to stop." Stop the music and call out, "Freeze!" After a few times, omit the warning and instead give children the challenge of finding a place on the inside or outside to the count of three after the music stops.

Before you start, have a small group of three or four children demonstrate moving into a hoop or shape without pushing or bumping.

3 Once children are familiar with this game, try introducing phrases from other languages. In Spanish, *inside/outside* is *adentro/afuera*, and in French, *dedans/dehors*. Invite children to con-

34

LANGUAGE ARTS

Resources

BOOKS
Big and Little, Up and Down: Early Concepts of Size and Direction by Ethel S. Berkley. HarperCollins, 1950.

MUSIC
"De Colores" ("All the Colors"), *Papa's Dream*. Music for Little People. Los Lobos.

tribute words from other languages they know, and add them to the Place in Space word chart for future use.

4 End the lesson in a calming and orderly way by having children return to their seats or get on line according to the color of their hoop, paper shape, or rug square. For example, "Reds can walk to their seats, greens can tiptoe to get on line." This provides a smooth transition from the liveliness of movement to the next activity.

Extending the Lesson

Use colors as cues. For example, direct children to find or share a yellow hoop (or paper shape or rug square). This is also a great way to learn the words for colors in other languages.

Assessment Checklist

Children learn new words very quickly when performing actions in connection with the meanings of the words (a popular technique also used in teaching children other languages). Here are some things to look for:

✹ Do children go to the correct place when you call "Inside" or "Outside"?

✹ To what extent can children learn and then use foreign language words meaning inside/outside?

LANGUAGE ARTS

Toys That Move

Using Action Words

Recreating the movements of a beloved childhood toy, a jack-in-the-box, children link words to action. By naming and using specific body parts in a creative movement exercise, they enjoy vocabulary and anatomy lessons.

Materials

* drum, triangle, or taped music
* masking tape
* picture of or actual jack-in-the-box (optional)

Warm-Up

Discuss with children toys that move. Ask questions, such as "What parts of the toys move? What sets them in motion? What are some of your favorite toys that move?" After your discussion, ask children if they can guess what toy you're imitating as you mime the motions of a jack-in-the-box. Ask them what parts of their bodies they can use to fold up like a jack-in-the-box. Have them practice folding up all parts of their arms from fingers to elbows and up to shoulders. Can they name all the parts that are foldable? You might like to make a simple diagram of an arm and label all the foldable parts they call

Language Arts

out: fingertips, knuckles, wrists, elbows, and shoulders (which fold by hunching forward).

This exercise can turn into an anatomy lesson if you continue by including foldable parts of the legs, torso, and spine. Some young children do not know all the names of body parts and the ways in which they move (their range of motion). This lesson gives them a fun and lively way to learn more about them.

Creative Movement

1 The fun of a jack-in-the-box is in the sudden way it pops out from a still, compact shape. Encourage children to recreate this surprise by folding up tightly and then quickly jumping out of their "box." Inform them that each child will have his or her own space, or box, to be in for the movement exercise. Urge them to listen carefully to the action words you speak. These words will set their toy in motion. But each time, the "jack" will do something different—hop, jump, spin, or dance. And when the jacks go back into their boxes, they will fold down in a special way. Children will need to concentrate on matching the name of the body part you call out and on folding it up tightly, until all parts are folded down to the floor.

2 Prepare a space for each child by putting a small piece of masking tape on the floor to mark each box. Ask children

LANGUAGE ARTS

to sit on them. When the drumbeat or music begins, remind everyone to fold up into the smallest shape possible, heads, arms, and legs tucked in. Call out or sing this little chant:

> The jack-in-the-box is folded up,
> Nobody knows it's there.
> It sits very quietly until
> All of a sudden it opens its top
> And jumps right out in the air.
> (or *hops, runs, tiptoes, gallops, dances*)

Remind children that they should keep going in the same direction without bumping the other jacks and listen for the signal to stop (a break in the music or a last sharp drumbeat). Then they must freeze.

3 After the jacks have frozen for a moment, ask them to quietly walk back to their boxes and reach their hands up to the ceiling as high as possible. Then name each body part to be folded up, beginning with the fingers and using the words children contributed during the warm-up discussion.

LANGUAGE ARTS

Resources

BOOKS
The Marvelous Toy by Tom Paxton. Morrow Junior Books, 1996.

Toys. Dorling Kindersley, 1993.

MUSIC
The Toy Symphony. Joseph Hayden.

To help recreate the motions of a toy, ask children to use sharp little mechanical movements. Or break the motion into beats: "Fold up your fingers, one-two-three. Fold up your wrists, one-two-three," and so on. You can count the beats on the drum. End with folding up the knees and ankles and, finally, folding down into the box. Once all the jacks are back in their boxes, start the chant again, but each time change the kind of movement they have to do: jump out, run out, dance out (encourage children to dance with one or two others). Try out six to eight different movements.

4 To end the lesson, have the jacks fold into their box one last time. Then give each a tap in turn and let them show the other children their favorite way of moving out of the box. They'll hop, crawl, or gallop back to their desks, the meeting area, or to get on line.

Extending the Lesson

Ask children to bring in a favorite toy and recreate its movements. Begin by asking children how their toy works or what it can do (for instance, a stuffed animal or doll can move its limbs or sleep). Have each child, or the class as a whole, imitate these motions.

Choose four or five students, each with different toy motions to share, and have them sit in a row. Tell them that they are toys on the shelf in a toy store. Have another child be the customer. As the customer touches each "toy," the toy comes to life and demonstrates its motions.

Assessment Checklist

This lesson helps children understand specific body parts and how they move. They also learn to respond to sound cues for performing certain motions. Imagination comes into play when they find ways to depict the actions of their toys. Here's what to look for:

* Can children notice and use all their joints for folding motions?
* Can children coordinate motions with sound cues?
* Optional: Can children successfully imitate the motion of their toy?

LANGUAGE ARTS

A Snail's Story

Folktales Come Alive

This Hawaiian folktale about friendship and loyalty tells the story of the relationship between tree snails and brown birds. It is meant to be told aloud, with the kind of lively engagement between teller and listener that makes folktales such an effective way to engage children in language arts.

Materials

* drum or taped music
* sheet or large piece of fabric
* tables and chairs (optional)

Warm-Up

Introduce children to the idea that animals can be friends who depend on each other. Give some examples, such as the cattle egret and the water buffalo. The egret, a beautiful white bird, eats the insects that bite the buffalo. Thus, each animal benefits from the other. Ask if anyone knows of other examples. (If possible, share a book about symbiotic relationships. See Resources, page 44.)

Language Arts

Now tell students they will hear a story about another animal friendship, that between Hawaiian snails and birds. (See page 43.) Add that in real life, snails and birds really do help each other, and that this folktale was made up to try to explain why.

You can also teach students some Hawaiian words from the tale:

tree snail = kahuli (kah-HOO-lee)
brown bird = kolea (koh-LAY-ah
forest fern = akolea (ah-koh-LAY-ah)

Creative Movement

1 Ask children which parts of the story they would like to act out. Help them recall the sequence of events, and discuss the special movement qualities of each creature. For instance, snails slowly slide along, flat on the ground. When frightened, they pull back inside their shells and, when the danger is over, cautiously re-emerge. Birds, on the other hand, swoop and perch, flutter when they bathe, and tuck their heads under their wings to sleep. Let children practice some of these motions while sitting in one place. Now, with a repertoire of motions, they can begin to recreate the story.

2 Designate the boundaries of the forest area in an open space in the room. Spread the sheet or piece of fabric on the floor to simulate the ferns. If feasible, arrange a few chairs to represent the trees. Play some slow music (or tap the drum) so children can explore the forest environment from the snails' point of view, sliding along with bodies flat on the ground and slithering around or over obstacles like trees. Give a signal (hand clap or drumbeat) for snails to pull inside their shells when frightened and another signal for them to come back out slowly. Let children practice sleeping like snails by pulling inside the shell (rolling up into a tight ball), then waking and going for a sip of water to the ferns.

LANGUAGE ARTS

3 Now give the entire group a chance to cover the same territory as birds. Have them use gliding, soaring, and flapping motions for flying, and hopping movements for perching on a branch or landing on the ground. Tell them the ferns are where the birds fluff their wings and then fill them with water.

4 Expand students' ability to observe movements and find words for them by making comments, such as "I'm watching Linda keep both arms spread out wide as she soars through the branches" or "Jared has a nice, tightly curled shape for a sleeping snail."

5 Have children recreate the whole story. Start them off by doing a brief version yourself. Then divide the class into two groups, snails and birds (they will switch roles later). Begin the story with the snails moving slowly along the ground and the birds perched up in the trees. Give a signal to indicate that the rain is falling, and have both snails and birds meet near the cloth. With snails sipping and birds fluffing feathers, children can imagine this as a place to make friends.

LANGUAGE ARTS

A Snail's Story

Once, on the beautiful island of Hawaii, trees, flowers, and ferns grew all around. Snails lived on the ground, and little brown birds flew happily through the trees. Every day, the afternoon rain fell and left a lovely mist floating through the forest. Then the snails (*kahuli*) came out to drink the sweet water dripping from the ferns (*akolea*). At the same time, the birds (*kolea*) flew down to take a bath in the wet ferns. Because the snails and birds met here every day, they became friends.

One day an enormous ship landed, with great white sails like no one had ever seen. The people from the boat had never seen a place as beautiful as Hawaii. They tromped around without looking where they were going and crushed many poor snails that had crawled out for their afternoon drink of water. Snails cried out to each other to hurry to safety. The little brown birds squawked and swooped over the heads of the strange people, trying to drive them away. Finally, the birds called out to the snails to climb up the trees to be safe. This is how the Hawaiian snails became tree snails.

That night, the snails in the trees began to cry. They were afraid they would die up there without the rainwater from the fern plants. The brown birds had an idea: They would fly down to the ferns after the afternoon rain, fill their feathers with extra water drops, and fly back up into the trees where they would shake the water onto the snails.

The next day, the snails got their first shower from the brown birds. Out of sheer happiness and gratitude, one snail started humming a lovely tune that echoed throughout the forest. Soon another snail and then another joined in until the entire forest was full of their beautiful sound. The brown birds usually had trouble getting to sleep. But that night, as they listened to the snails' humming, they tucked their heads under their wings and dozed right off. Perhaps if you listen very quietly, you will hear the snails and fall asleep too.

LANGUAGE ARTS

Resources

BOOKS
The Biggest House in the World by Leo Lionni. Knopf, 1968.

Can We Be Friends? Nature's Partners by Alexandra Wright. Charlesbridge, 1994.

The Snail's Spell by Joanne Ryder. Puffin Books, 1982.

MUSIC
Hawaiian music by the artists Keola Beamer, Slack-key Guitar, and The Brothers Cazimero.

6 Ask a couple of children to take the role of the strangers who tromp through the forest. Perhaps one of the birds can call out, "Snails, come up here with us in the trees and be safe." As they become more familiar with the story, children can take on more of the dialogue. They may cry out, "We snails need water or we'll dry up." Birds can answer, "Let's fill our feathers with water and fly up to share it with the snails." Make sure only one snail starts the humming, but then encourage the rest of the snails to join in. The birds then tuck in their heads one by one until they are all "asleep." Have the snails and birds switch roles and repeat the story.

7 Ask children to share their thoughts about being a snail or a bird. Or ask what ways friends helped each other in this story. Then discuss how children help each other in school. You may want to chart their ideas for display in class. Another idea is to have some children take turns telling parts of the story while others act it out.

Extending the Lesson

Invite students to draw pictures of and write about their favorite parts of the story. Put all the material into a class book titled "The Snails' Story." If you take pictures of children acting out the story, add them to the book too, alongside children's drawings of those actions.

Assessment Checklist

Stories like folktales offer children many ways of engaging their imagination and using expressive movements. Here they also enact a story about friendship and caring. Some things to notice:

* Can children use expressive motions to stay in character when playing the roles of both the snails and the birds?
* To what extent do children focus on and engage each other in acting out the relationship between the snails and the birds?

LANGUAGE ARTS

Whirl, Whirl!

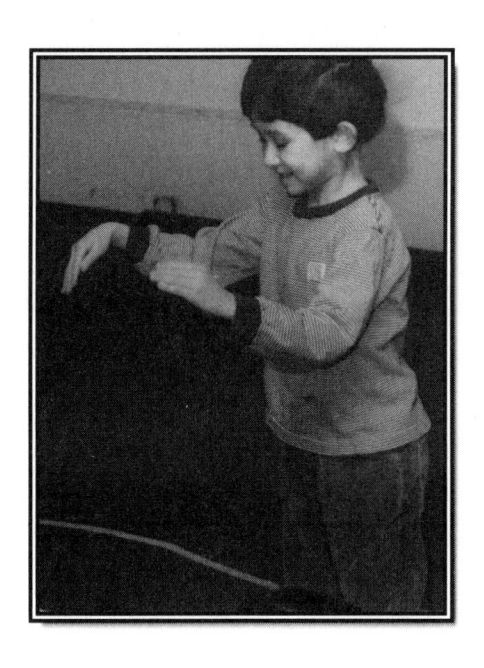

Poetry in Motion

Words come alive as children interpret this inspiring Langston Hughes poem through sound and movement. Finding motions to express ideas deepens children's ability to recreate what they know and feel.

Materials

- drum, triangle, and/or taped music
- masking tape

Optional:
- scarves or pieces of fabric
- *Coming Home* (see Resources, page 49)

Warm-Up

Suggest to students that poems help us think about ordinary things in new ways. When people write poetry, they want us to experience a new feeling or idea about something we already know—for instance, night, day, playing, and whirling. Tell children about Langston Hughes (1902–1967), an African-American poet who lived

45

Language Arts

mostly in New York City. (If feasible, read or show pictures from *Coming Home*, a biography of Hughes by Floyd Cooper.) Then ask students to close their eyes and listen to Hughes's poem "Dream Variation":

> To fling my arms wide
> In some place of the sun,
> To whirl and to dance
> Till the white day is done.
> Then rest at cool evening
> Beneath a tall tree
> While night comes on gently,
>   Dark like me—
> That is my dream!

When you finish, ask children to share ideas or ask questions about what they heard. Ask if someone will demonstrate his or her idea of whirling or resting. Point out that in the poem, there are very active times and also quiet, gentle, resting times. Brainstorm with children ideas about when they are active or resting during the day, whether at home or at school. These ideas will serve as raw material for imaginative movements later on.

Creative Movement

1. Set the stage for a whirl in the park. Put pieces of masking tape on the floor in a cleared space in the classroom where the "trees" are to stand. Half the group will be trees and half "whirlers" (later they will switch roles). The trees take their places and freeze into a shape, holding their arms in interesting ways to form branches. Give the trees scarves or fabric pieces to use as leaves; they can wave these in the wind or let them hang to shelter resting children.

2. Have the whirlers stand on one side of the room and enter the "park" one at a time, flinging their arms around and whirling as you read the poem. Your signal for them to start can be turning on soft music (or gently beating the drum) as you begin to read aloud.

LANGUAGE ARTS

3 Give children time to respond to each new phrase and idea of the poem. Encourage them to take their time moving while you read. For instance, when you read "To fling my arms wide/In some place of the sun," they can stretch and reach with their arms as fully as possible, maybe even jumping up as they do so.

4 Stop the music (or beat the drum sharply) and ask the whirlers to freeze and then walk over to a tree. Read the lines "Then rest at cool evening/Beneath a tall tree...," and ask the whirlers to relax their bodies (to a count of 10) as they slowly assume a lying-down position.

5 After a few moments of silence, ask children to sit up and share their experiences of being the trees or the whirlers. Questions you might ask are: "What did you like about your part? What were some favorite motions you used? What would you like to add for next time?" Then have children switch roles and repeat the exercise.

LANGUAGE ARTS

Extending the Lesson

Try adding a homemade rhythm band to keep a beat for the whirlers. Children learn to be good observers when they can coordinate sounds to the motions their classmates are making. Select three students to make one of each of the three instruments listed in "Shake, Rattle, and Roll" (see below). Each instrument makes a distinctive sound, which you can discuss with the students. Once you have dancers, a poet/narrator, and musicians, invite children from other classrooms or parents to come to a performance.

Shake, Rattle, and Roll

Shake: Construct a tambourine by stapling together the edges of two paper plates, making sure to leave a small opening. Drop dried beans and/or rice into the opening, then staple it closed. Decorate the plate with paint, crayons, or markers, and crepe-paper streamers. A child can shake or tap this instrument to get a good sound.

LANGUAGE ARTS

Resources

BOOKS
The Block: Poems by Langston Hughes selected by Lowery S. Sims. Viking, 1995.

Coming Home by Floyd Cooper. Putnam, 1994.

"Dream Variation," in *I Am the Darker Brother*, an anthology edited by Arnold Adoff. Macmillan, 1968.

MUSIC
Uptown. Duke Ellington. Columbia Jazz Masterpieces.

Rattle: Pour a teaspoon of rice through the opening of a medium-sized balloon. Then blow up the balloon and tie a firm knot. A child can hold the end of the balloon and shake it vigorously. For a handle, he or she can twist a rubber band around the knot.

Roll: Fill an empty juice or coffee can with beans, buttons, or gravel. Seal the opening with contact paper and tape. Cover the instrument with construction paper and draw or paint designs. A child can roll this instrument along the floor (or even shake it) to produce a lively sound.

Assessment Checklist

Through the power of poetry, children can be inspired to create expressive motions. This activity also emphasizes contrasting movement qualities that reflect contrasting elements in the poem. As they watch each other perform, children see words come alive. Here are some things to look for:

* In what ways does a child use his or her body to express the words in the poem?
* Are children able to engage in both active (fling, whirl) and still (resting) activities?

LANGUAGE ARTS

Obstacle Course Search

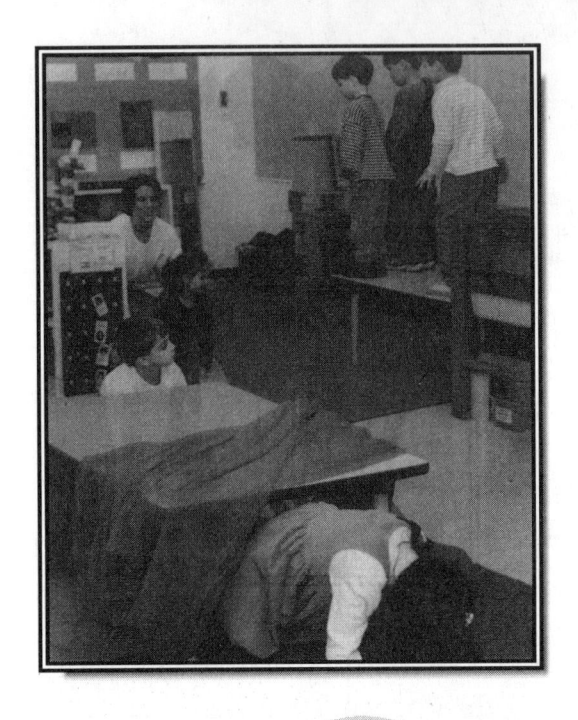

Finding the Words

As they go on an exciting search to find a rare lost bird, children expand their vocabulary by linking words to actions.

Materials

- classroom furniture
- taped music
- an object to represent a lost bird
- sheet or piece of fabric (optional)

Warm-Up

Tell students a story about getting a call from the local zoo asking for help in finding a lost rare bird. Describe going on an imaginary search over mountains, down steep ravines, through raging rivers, squeezing through tunnels until you reach a place where you can silently search for this shy bird. Ask for daring volunteers to come

LANGUAGE ARTS

along. Set the stage by designating the search area and rearranging classroom furniture if possible (or using equipment in the gym or some other large space). Children can help construct the geography. Ask for their ideas on what furniture to use for mountains, tunnels, or rivers. Tell them they will have to negotiate the obstacle course until you decide they have reached the place where they can begin their search for a hidden object that represents the bird.

Creative Movement

Set chairs next to tables so children can climb up, crawl over, and get down the other side of the "mountains." A table or series of chairs set close together can serve as a tunnel, with a sheet or piece of fabric draped on top. Put a long strip of masking tape along the floor to represent a tightrope across a raging river. Ask for a few volunteers to help set up the course. Then, as other children watch, talk them through the series of obstacles. Have them first "scale steep mountains," then "crawl or slither through tunnels," and finally "balance along the rope bridge." Make a chart of the action words used. Ask children to name other action words to add to the chart.

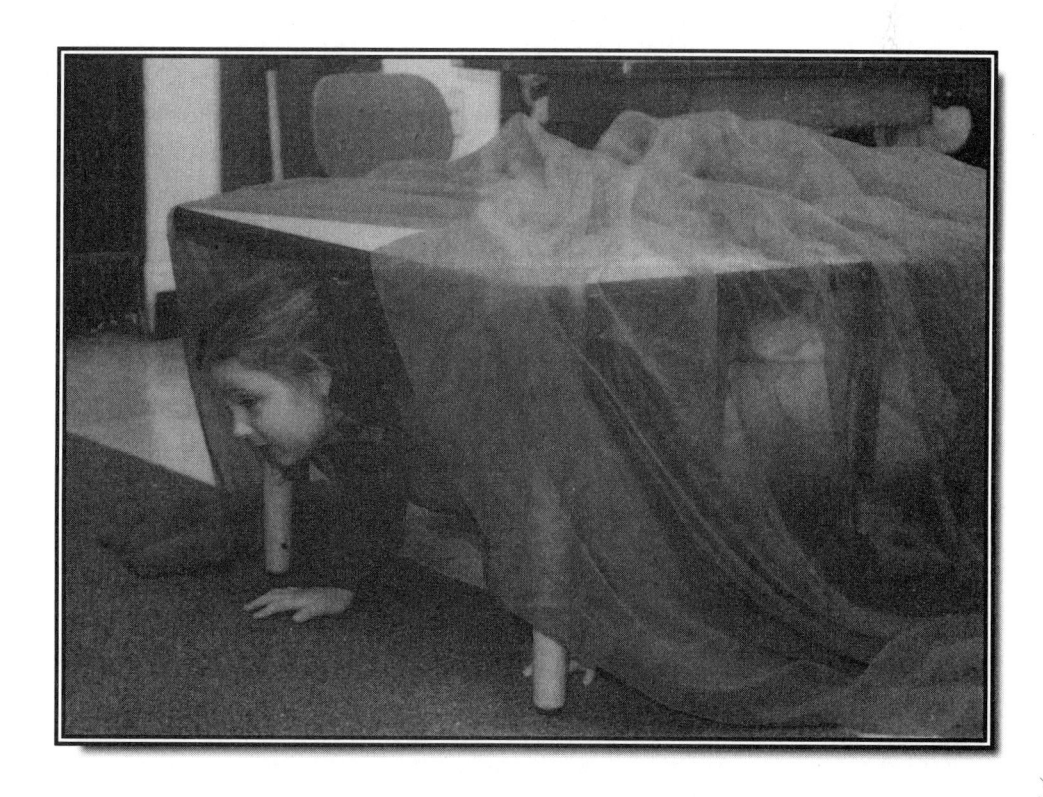

LANGUAGE ARTS

2 Once the obstacle course is set up (including the placement of the lost bird), put on the music and have children go through the course one by one. Challenge them to repeat the course going forward, backward, and sideways. Occasionally, have everyone stop and watch one person's particular way of going. Provide a running commentary, using a variety of words to describe the action: "Look how Keisha is slithering slowly down the mountain." Ask children to name any new words they heard, and add them to the word chart.

3 After all children have done the obstacle course three times, gather them together in a circle and announce it is time to search for the lost bird. Give children instructions about areas to look in, and warn them to search very quietly so they don't frighten the bird away. Tell them to just point when they find the bird, and you will retrieve it. Once you have done so, let children wave goodbye to the bird before you return it to the "zoo."

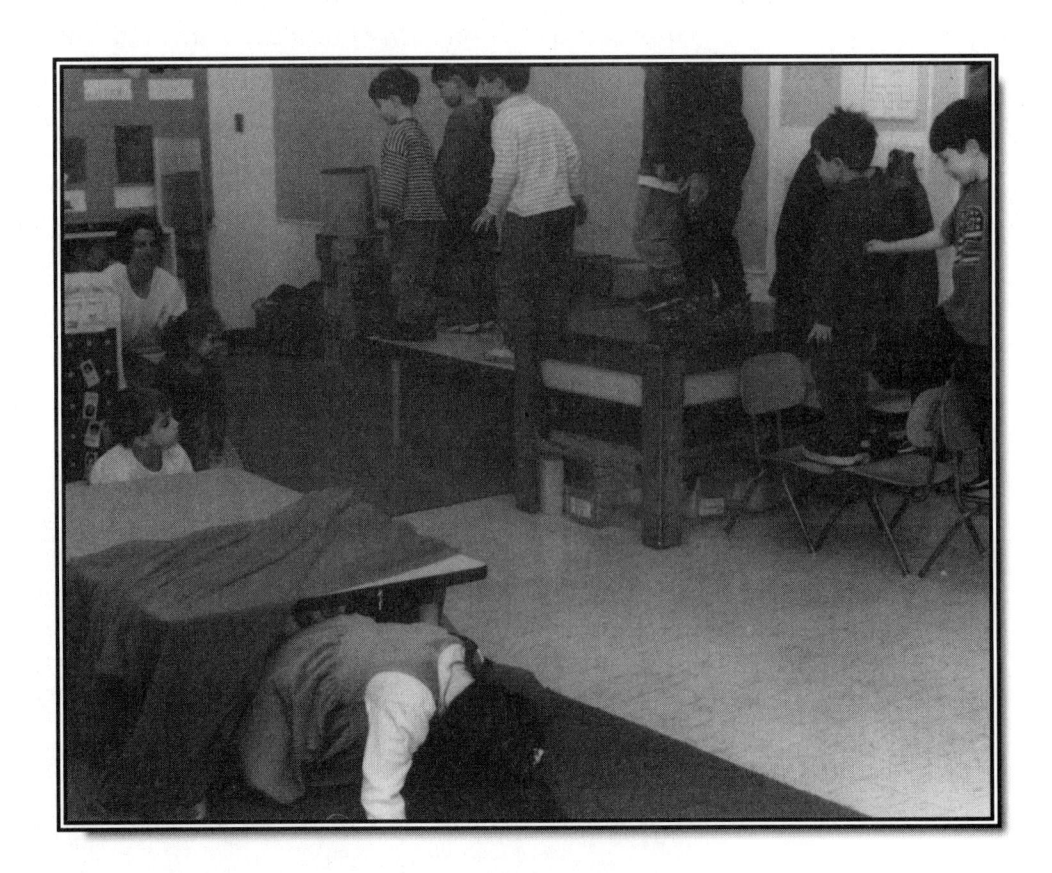

LANGUAGE ARTS

Resources

BOOKS
Can You Walk the Plank? by June Behrens. Children's Press, 1976.

MUSIC
"Beach Fire Dancers," *Rhythm*. Govi. Real Music, 1997.

Extending the Lesson

Put action words to use in a new way by asking children to design the obstacle course. Tell them to create four obstacles/areas to be used for climbing, crawling, balancing, and sliding, respectively. Then divide the class into four groups, with each group putting together one obstacle course with designated equipment. When all this is accomplished, ask one member of each group to demonstrate how to use their obstacle course. Then proceed with the search.

Assessment Checklist

Children learn about another dimension to words when they must link them to actions and spaces. Here's what to watch for:

* Can children devise different ways of using the same piece of equipment?
* What are all the ways children can find to describe how and where they perform an action on the obstacle course?
* Are children able to follow your instructions and demonstration for traversing the obstacle course?

SOCIAL STUDIES

The Circus
People Who Work With Animals

As children learn to create exciting circus animal tricks, they also learn that caring for the animals is an equally important part of the work of trainers.

Materials

- rulers, dowels, or other kind of sticks for half the class
- taped music or drum

Optional:

- chair
- colored plastic hoops (see Resources, page 20)
- *The Magic Ring: A Year With the Big Apple Circus* (see Resources, page 57)

Warm-Up

Ask children what they know about how people work with circus animals. Stimulate the discussion by asking "How do animals learn tricks from people? How do trainers get animals to understand them? What do animals need from people in order to live and work in the circus?" Chart children's ideas for use in the movement activity. (If feasible, enrich the lesson by reading from *The Magic Ring*.

SOCIAL STUDIES

Focus on the section on trainers and animals, their work together, and how both have families who live and work in the circus.)

Creative Movement

1 Discuss how the trainer cares for the animal and makes sure it eats nutritious food and has a clean, comfortable place to live and sleep. Explain that the trainer also gives the animal treats when it does a good job. Stress that the trainer must use clear hand signals so the animal can understand what to do.

To demonstrate this, have a child take the part of the trainer, hold up the stick (or dowel or ruler), and make a hand motion that indicates to the "animal" that it should jump over the stick. Then ask the trainer to make a motion for the animal to crawl underneath the stick. Another hand motion can include putting the stick on the floor and using a finger to draw circles around it so that the animal knows it should run in circles around the stick. As children watch, help the demonstrating student create hand motions indicating that the animal should jump up, sit, roll over, and take a bow. To increase children's awareness of how unique different species are, choose two animals with contrasting qualities for the movement exercises—for example, a monkey and a lion.

2 To begin, introduce the idea of staying in character. This means that a child needs to imagine how the animal or the trainer

SOCIAL STUDIES

would behave under all circumstances and try to portray both physical actions and facial expressions. A monkey might screech, then crouch down and scamper around in a circle, while a lion could roar, then prowl back and forth in a slower, more stately way. A trainer would always use hand gestures to direct the animal and then give it treats for good work. Point out such differences, and encourage children to use descriptive language. You might comment, "I am seeing lions crouch down and then spring through the hoop. Monkeys are scuttling down from the chair and grooming themselves." Linking actions to words is a great way to build a vivid vocabulary.

3 Ask students to choose partners and decide who will be the animal and who the trainer (they will switch later). Then have each pair sit in spaces you designate, together with their sticks. (Note: If you can use a chair, you can provide more variety for jumping, climbing, and crawling.)

4 Now put on the music or play the drum. Ask trainers to have their animals do four or five tricks. Remind trainers to give their animals

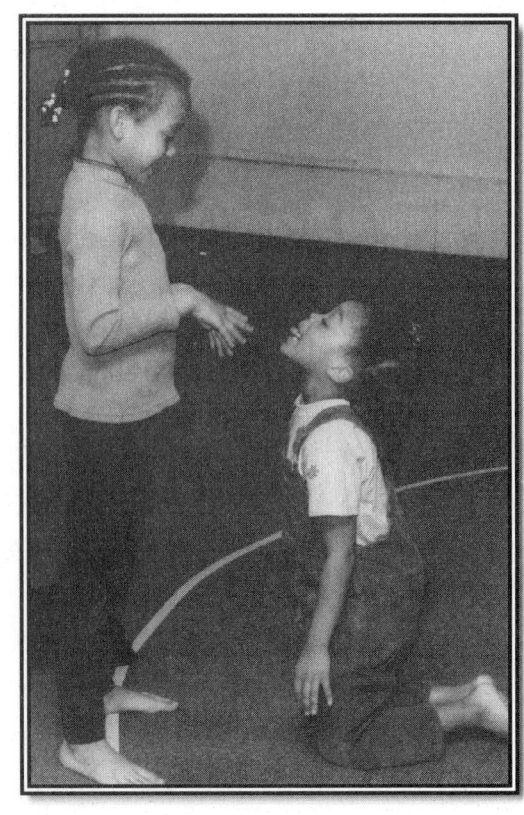

SOCIAL STUDIES

Resources

BOOKS
If I Ran the Circus by Dr. Seuss. Random House, 1956.

Madeline and the Gypsies by Ludwig Bemelmans. Viking, 1959, 1987.

The Magic Ring: A Year With the Big Apple Circus by Hana Machotka. William Morrow, 1988.

MUSIC
Mod Marches. Hap Palmer. Educational Activities, Inc.

pretend treats for good work, and remind the animals to watch the trainers' signals carefully. Then have the partners switch roles. After one or two switches, ask some of the more creative pairs to demonstrate their circus acts to the rest of the class. Encourage the audience to watch for new ideas they can use later on.

5 Conclude the lesson by asking the trainers to share their strategies for teaching the animal their signals. Ask them how it felt to be the animal and then the trainer and what they learned. Which was their favorite role and why? If children are interested or have questions, consider writing to your local circus for more information (and be sure to send along some pictures of your animals and trainers).

Extending the Lesson

Share the animal and trainer acts with other classes and/or with parents by putting on a show. For simple, easy-to-remove makeup, use water soluble crayons such as Aquarelle®. Create a lion with a brown nose and whiskers. A ringmaster can have colorful stars on his or her cheeks and forehead. Prepare a batch of tickets and bags of popcorn, and let the show begin! Invite the audience to ask the animals and trainers questions about their act at the end.

Assessment Checklist

In this activity, children learn how to stay in character, either as trainer or animal. You may want to notice whether

* children's movements and gestures clearly convey the qualities of their animal (are the monkeys light and bouncy? the lions stately and menacing?).
* the trainers give clear hand signals and adapt their demands to their animals' abilities.
* children participate in both roles.

SOCIAL STUDIES

The Ghanaian Talking Drum

Sounds From Another Culture

In this exercise, children learn about a special Ghanaian drum that "talks" in order to send messages. In an adaptation of this custom, they will learn to match the movements of their feet with the sound messages from the drum.

Materials

* drum

Warm-Up

Have children sit on the floor in a circle as you explain the talking drum. Tell them the drum hangs from a string around a player's neck. He or she beats it on one side with one hand and rubs the other side with a stick. The result is a sound like a person's voice. In Ghana, everyone knows what the different variations in this sound mean. Tell children that we can take this idea and create our own sounds. The drum is a copycat and matches its beats to the sound our feet make when we walk, gallop, tiptoe, jump, or stomp. You can chant, "When your feet do the walking, the drum does the talking."

SOCIAL STUDIES

Creative Movement

1 Ask a volunteer to walk around the circle while children listen for the rhythm of his or her feet. Pick up the beat on your drum and lead the chant. With a sharp bang on the drum, signal the student to stop and return to his or her place in the circle. Then ask another volunteer to gallop around the group. Pick up that rhythm on the drum, too. Continue with other volunteers tiptoeing, stomping, running, and jumping while you create a different beat for each gait.

2 With everyone still seated, run through the different beats you created. Ask children to identify which beat stands for which gait. Explain that in the next part of the game, they will be matching various gaits with their beats.

3 Have children stand up and, as they concentrate on your drumbeat message, start moving in the same direction without bumping each other. Begin with a walking beat. As children get into the rhythm, switch the beat to tiptoeing, galloping, or running. After three changes, hit the drum sharply for "Stop." Children will enjoy the challenge of matching the right gait to the right beat and stopping before they're "caught" still moving after the drum signals to stop. Add variety by giving more changes or sudden stops and starts.

SOCIAL STUDIES

Resources

BOOKS
Beating the Drum by Josephine Parker. Millbrook Press, 1992.

My Drum by Kay Davies and Wendy Oldfield. G. Stevens, 1994.

Patakin: World Tales of Drums and Drummers by Nina Jaffee. Henry Holt, 1994.

Talking Drums of Africa by Christine Price. Charles Scribner's Sons, 1973.

MUSIC
Drums of Passion. Baba Olatunji. Columbia Records.

4 Now make a "Dance Soup" by repeating a drum sequence. This lets children experience creating a real dance. Solicit their suggestions for putting together the sequence. They might, for instance, decide to start with tiptoe, add galloping and stomping, then end with jumps. Ask them to do the sequence in a follow-the-leader line. Or have them change direction for each gait: gallop north, tiptoe south, stomp east, and jump west. Afterward, have them form small groups of three to four and create their own sequences.

Extending the Lesson

Ask children to make up their own steps/gaits and matching drumbeats. They might scratch a circle on the drum with a fingernail to indicate spinning or bang slowly to signal giant, dinosaur-like steps. You can post a list of these. You can also write them on pieces of paper, fold them up, toss them in a bowl, and have a student pick one out for a drummer (you or a student) to follow.

Assessment Checklist

Being able to coordinate movement and sound is one of the basic elements of creative moment. Here are some things to notice:

* To what extent can children coordinate their motions with the rhythm of the drum?

* Can students remember the whole sequence of dance steps in the "Dance Soup" activity?

SOCIAL STUDIES

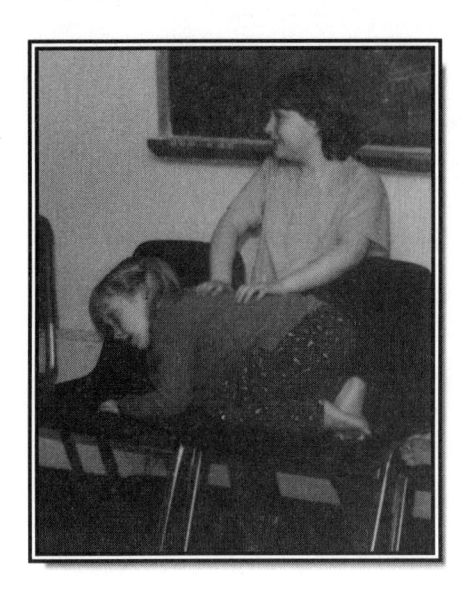

Pack Up the Produce!

Where Our Food Comes From

In a lively re-creation of what goes on in a grocery store, children learn to cooperate while experiencing the roles of workers and their relationship to the produce.

Materials

- taped music or drum
- classroom furniture
- large garbage bags
- paper and drawing materials

Warm-Up

Young children can visit a grocery store to understand where the fruits and vegetables on their tables or in their lunch boxes come from. Such a visit will allow them to see how workers unload produce, sort, package, and display it, price, sell, and bag it. In advance,

SOCIAL STUDIES

arrange with the store manager a time for children to interview the workers. Prepare trip sheets for children to fill out. Let them know that after their trip, they will create their own grocery store.

Creative Movement

1 Ask children to use their trip sheets or memories to draw one part of the fruit or vegetable preparation process, including what the workers are doing. They can add written comments at the bottom of the page. You may get drawings of unloading, throwing out bad produce, neatly stacking or packaging produce, pricing it, or selling and bagging it. Have a discussion in which children share their drawings and then arrange them in the sequence from unloading to selling.

This is me and I'm standing next to the carts that are moving potatoes. And I'm looking at them moving it. —Francesca

2 Discuss with children what each job in the sequence entails. What do the workers need to do their job (forklifts or hand trucks, packaging machinery, sorting tables, paper or plastic bags, cash registers)? How do workers know when it is their turn to do something or what comes next? Make sure everyone understands all the steps of each process. Collect the drawings and put them together in a class book titled "Where Our Food Comes From."

SOCIAL STUDIES

3 Set up a re-creation of a grocery store using any available school furniture. A few chairs placed in a row can be the delivery truck; a table or a towel laid on the floor can be the sorting area. Put the garbage bags in a pile for bagging merchandise later. Ask children to help you decide where each thing goes and how it is going to be used.

4 Divide the class into two groups: (1) the fruits and/or vegetables and (2) the workers (later on, they will switch). Assign workers to each station of the grocery store. Make sure they understand how to perform their jobs in pantomime and can easily pass the fruits or vegetables along to the next station. Children acting as the produce wait at the loading station and fold themselves into potato, tomato, or apple shapes for rolling.

5 Signal the start by playing music or a drum. Workers carry or roll the produce to the sorting table or packaging machinery and then pass it on to the next station. When the fruits and vegetables finally arrive for bagging after being purchased, have the "produce" children get into a garbage bag with their heads sticking out.
Safety Note: Caution children never to put a plastic bag over their nose or mouth.

SOCIAL STUDIES

Resources

BOOKS
A Fruit and Vegetable Man by Roni Schotter. Little Brown & Co., 1993.

The Raffi Singable Songbook by Raffi. Crown Publishers, Inc., 1980.

What's It Like to Be a Grocer by Shelley Wilks. Troll Associates, 1990.

MUSIC
The Corner Grocery Store. Raffi. MCA Records, Inc.

6 Before you have the groups switch roles, ask children to talk about their roles and how things might run better. For instance, some children might say that the produce was coming to them too quickly and piling up. Suggest that someone assume the role of manager to keep things moving along and control the flow of produce coming to the stations. This enactment will give children a firsthand experience of what real workers have to deal with.

Extending the Lesson

If possible, arrange a trip to a farm or a produce packaging factory. Then have children put on a similar re-enactment. Share what children learned with parents or other students. Children can read from their class book, Where Our Food Comes From, and take questions from the audience. Or you can narrate as students recreate their grocery store, farm, or packaging factory.

Assessment Checklist

Children begin to understand the world around them by observing how people carry out their work activities. In re-creating them, children connect what they see with what they know and can do. They also realize they must be aware of each other and cooperate in order to get their work done. Here's what to look for:

* Can students reconstruct a sequence of events easily?
* Do students respond cooperatively to classmates and carry out their part of the job?
* Can students comfortably switch roles from produce to worker?

SOCIAL STUDIES

Become a Machine

Learning How Things Work

By acting out the workings of a machine, children learn the role it plays in their lives as well as the motions the machine makes in operation. This game provides a valuable exercise in observation and cooperation.

Materials

* taped music or drum
* chart paper
* recommended books (optional, see Resources, page 69)

Warm-Up

Machines are everywhere: the electric toothbrush, washing machine, or toaster we use at home; on the street, a cement mixer, crane, steam shovel, or jackhammer. Each machine has a particular shape and uses a certain sequence of movements to do its work.

Have children brainstorm all the machines they can think of in

SOCIAL STUDIES

the home, in the classroom, on the street, or in other places (such as an amusement park). Chart their ideas. Discuss the qualities machines have in common: needing to be turned on and off, clicking or humming, using energy (gasoline or electricity). Taking a toaster as an example, ask children to help you reconstruct its use—putting in the bread, pushing down the plunger, pulling out the toast that pops up. Chart the sequence to help them remember what to do should they re-create the toaster in their movement activity.

Creative Movement

Begin by choosing and discussing one of the machines suggested by children in the warm-up. Ask, "What are the main parts of this machine that make it work? How do the parts work together? What comes first? What comes next? How do you turn it on and off?"

SOCIAL STUDIES

2 After the discussion, ask children how many of them will be needed to make up this machine. Ask for volunteers to enact each machine part. For example, if you choose to act out a steam shovel, the players will take on the parts of the engine cab, the shovel, the whistle, or any other part they think is important. When you have all the "pieces" together, be sure each child knows what his or her part is supposed to be and when in the sequence the work occurs. Then "turn on" the machine by playing music or a drum. Have the rest of the class watch. Afterward, invite them to give comments to and ask questions of the players. Then have each child choose a machine to "build" with a few other students.

3 After children choose their machines, divide the class into groups of two or three (or however many are needed for a particular machine). Each group decides how to put its machine together. Let each group practice its machine and then present it to

SOCIAL STUDIES

the entire class, who will guess what machine it is. Encourage the audience to ask questions or make comments about how the machine works. Also solicit suggestions for improving the way it works.

4 Once all the machines have had a turn—and a critique—have the groups try out revisions or new ideas for their machines. Ask children to suggest machine "rules," and chart them: machines turn on and off, they have connected parts, and the parts work in a certain sequence.

5 When you repeat this activity on another day, ask students to choose a machine from each of three categories—home, school, and street—and try them all. Encourage children to invent their own machines to replace machines that, for example, mix cement, steamroll the road, or brush teeth. These invented machines are sure to entertain but must still obey all the rules of real working machines.

SOCIAL STUDIES

Resources

BOOKS

Machines and How They Work by David Burnie. Dorling Kindersley, 1991.

Mike Mulligan and His Steam Shovel by Virginia Lee Burton. Houghton Mifflin, 1939.

The Way Things Work by David Macaulay. Houghton Mifflin, 1998.

MUSIC

"Take Me Riding in My Car," *Songs to Grow On.* Woodie Guthrie.

Extending the Lesson

Enrich children's understanding of machines by arranging for them to talk to people who operate them. Invite a school custodian to demonstrate the waxing machine or a cafeteria worker to show children the dishwasher. Ask a parent to share something small from home, a power tool or kitchen appliance. When children reenact these machines, be sure to discuss the role of the machine operator and have someone act that part too.

Safety Note: Remind children never to touch an electrical tool unless an adult is present.

Assessment Checklist

This lesson provides children with valuable instruction about the relationship between individual parts and the whole—especially how the parts must cooperate to make the whole work. Look for the following things:

* Can students identify a machine part and understand how it fits in with the other parts?
* To what extent can a child cooperate with other group members to create the machine?

SOCIAL STUDIES

Dragon Dance

Celebrating Chinese New Year

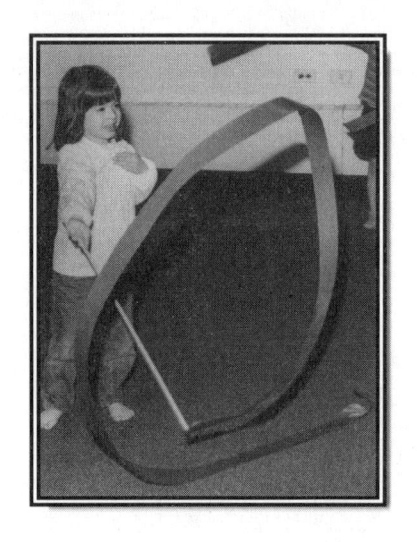

Chinese schoolchildren use ribbon sticks for fun, celebration, and physical coordination. Adult ribbon stick dancers are often part of the Chinese New Year parade honoring the Great Dragon, who brings everyone good luck for the new year. In this lesson, children acquire a new skill while learning about an important cultural celebration.

Materials

* drum
* ribbon stick for each child (see Resources, page 74, and Tip, below)
* recommended books (see Resources)
* long piece of fabric (optional)

Tip

If you don't have ribbon sticks, you can easily make them by winding the end of a pipe cleaner around two or three 24-inch crepe-paper streamers.

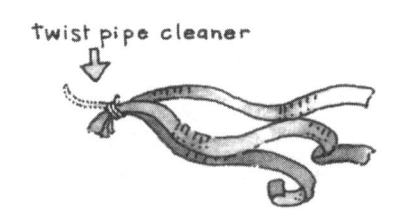

twist pipe cleaner

70

SOCIAL STUDIES

Warm-Up

Ask children what they know about New Year's celebrations. What do they have in common (preparations for a new start, rituals or customs that encourage good luck or prosperity, blessings for the coming year)? Tell students that during Chinese New Year (which comes six to eight weeks after January 1), Chinese children and their families celebrate both inside the home and outside on the streets of their community. Read aloud *The Dancing Dragon* (see Resources, page 74) to give them an understanding of the holiday as well as ideas they can use later when they reenact the New Year's parade.

Creative Movement

Discuss the role of the dragon in the New Year's celebration. Tell children that the dragon's fierceness scares away troubles, bad dreams, and other scary things. Therefore the dragon is the best creature to roar in good luck for the New Year. Ask children what they would like the dragon to scare away. Tell them later on they

SOCIAL STUDIES

will play the dragon themselves and scare away everything they have just mentioned.

2 Explain to children that the dragon is really a costume held up by dancers who move together in a line to make the dragon look real. (You might show them an illustration in one of the books. See Resources, page 74.)

3 Create your own dragon by designating one child as the head of the dragon. Call others up one by one to become part of the dragon's long, twisting body. They will hold on to the shirt or dress of the person in front of them. (If you have a long piece of fabric, turn it into the dragon's body by tossing it over the line of children.) When everyone is hooked up, have children prance up and down in place, doing the "dragon shuffle."

4 Lead the dragon around the room as you beat the drum. Add some excitement by asking for a big dragon roar on the count of three! End by signaling children to slowly settle down to the floor, still holding on to each other, to take a "dragon nap." Prepare them for the next part of the activity by asking each child to tiptoe to a meeting area when you give him/her a tap.

SOCIAL STUDIES

5 Tell children there are many elements in the parade that work to usher in the dragon and its good luck: floats, bands, and ribbon stick dancers. As children watch, take a ribbon stick and demonstrate how to use wide arm motions to make the ribbon part move freely. Sweep the stick back and forth overhead to make an arc like a rainbow. Make full arm circles overhead, then to the side, then do a figure eight with overhead swishes. Shake the stick rapidly up and down to make a "snake" or "writing in the air." Then give each child a ribbon stick and have children stand at least two feet apart so no one gets tangled up with or hits neighbors. With a drumbeat, signal them to start practicing all the motions you showed them. Encourage children to make up their own. Then create a sequence of four motions and have children repeat it: eight rainbows, eight circles, eight snakes, eight swishes.

SOCIAL STUDIES

Resources

BOOKS

The Dancing Dragon by Marcia Vaughan. Mondo, 1996.

Dragon Parade by Steven A. Chin. Steck-Vaughn, 1993.

Gung Hay Fat Choy: Happy New Year by June Behrens. Children's Press, 1982.

Happy New Year by Demi. Crown, 1997.

Lion Dancer: Ernie Wan's Chinese New Year by Kate Waters. Scholastic, 1991.

AUDIO/VISUAL

Big Bird in China. Sesame Street. Videocassette.

EQUIPMENT

Ribbon sticks. Toledo Physical Education Supply Co. 1-800-489-6256.

6 Divide the group so that half are ribbon stick dancers and half form the dragon. Have the dragon children stand to one side and watch the ribbon stick dancers perform. After a few sequences, ask the dancers to sit down and wait for the dragon to bring them good luck. The dragon enters, weaving in and out of the seated dancers. Every once in a while, signal the dragon to stop and roar on the count of three. Then have children switch roles and repeat the exercise. Afterward, ask children to share what they liked best about being the dragon and the dancer.

Our Chinese Dragon   —Ana

Extending the Lesson

Here's how to explore the dragon's qualities and powers: Have children sit on the floor with some space around each of them. Ask them to imagine they are dragons asleep in their mountaintop nests and that they are waking to the sound of firecrackers announcing Chinese New Year. Encourage them to stretch their wings and fly around the world (everyone moving in a clockwise direction to avoid bumping) to scare away anything that troubles children. When they spot something, such as a bad dream or a bully, let the dragons pounce and roar to scare them away. Signal the pouncing time with a sharp beat of the drum. After a few rounds, ask the dragons to share what things they scared away.

SOCIAL STUDIES

Assessment Checklist

This exercise requires children to focus on each other in two ways: playing with ribbon sticks safely, and staying attached in follow-the-leader style to create the dragon. Things to notice include:

* To what extent can students observe the demonstrations of ribbon stick skills and replicate them?
* Can children enjoy the excitement of being part of the dragon while cooperating and fulfilling their task?

This is me twirling my ribbon stick. —Hannah

MATH

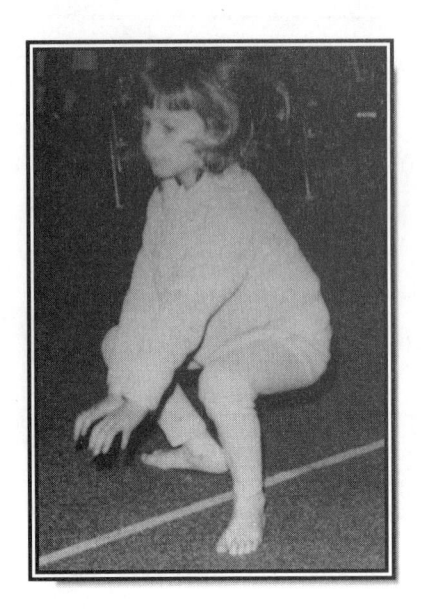

Jumping Numbers

Using Counting and Sequencing

Finding all the ways you can use your body to jump in time to a beat is an exciting way for children to learn to count and put together movement sequences.

Materials

- drum (or simply clap and count)
- masking tape
- *Quick as a Cricket* (optional, see Resources, page 79)

Warm-Up

Ask children to think about different animals that jump. Solicit volunteers to demonstrate animals that jump on different levels: a frog jumps on a low level, a rabbit on a medium level, a kangaroo on a high level. Discuss the differences and similarities between them and how moving on different levels changes the shape of the movement. Help children become better jumpers by pointing out how important it is to start and end jumps with their knees bent.

MATH

Now ask children to think of at least two ways that people jump. Have a couple of children demonstrate. Contrast human jumps with animal jumps. (The book *Quick as a Cricket* can help in this discussion.)

Creative Movement

1 Have children sit in a circle and take turns jumping all the way around the circle and back to their spot as you clap or keep time with the drum. Stimulate imaginations by asking children to suggest various animal jumps and human jumps. Suggest jumping jacks and jump-and-spin if no one thinks of them. Be sure the variety of jumps suggested includes some high ones (kangaroo or jumping jacks) and some low ones (frog jumps) in addition to the medium ones (rabbit jumps).

2 Have children practice five or six different kinds of jumps that you call out: "Let's count 10 jumps like a frog. Everyone go in the same direction. Now 10 jumping jacks! Now 10 jump-and-spins!"

MATH

3 Put several jumps together in a "Jump Soup." You have lots of good ingredients to choose from by now: frog and rabbit jumps, wiggly jumps, jumps that spin or go from side to side. Tell children they will repeat a sequence of five different jumps four times, going on the diagonal from one end of the room to the other. (Lay down a path with masking tape.) First, count out four beats so they can hear the rhythm and speed. Then have them jump one at a time. Keep a steady beat on the drum as you call out the jumps: "frog two-three-four, turn two-three-four, side-to-side two-three-four, rabbit two-three-four, jumping jacks two-three-four."

Extending the Lesson

Children learn more about movement when they can watch each other. Have half the group sit and watch the other half do the "Jump

MATH

Resources

BOOKS
Hop, Jump by Ellen Stoll Walsh. Harcourt Brace, 1993.

Quick as a Cricket by Audrey & Don Wood, Ingram. 1989.

MUSIC
"Jump Shamador" and "Shake It to the One You Love the Best."
Shake It to the One You Love the Best: Play Songs and Lullabies From Black Musical Traditions. Cheryl Warren-Mattox. Warren-Mattox Productions, 1989.

Soup." Then switch. When each soup group has finished, solicit comments or questions from the group watching.

Assessment Checklist

Children use their creativity by making up jumps and then arranging them in a "soup." They develop their sense of rhythm when they are required to jump once per beat. Things to look for include:

* Can children invent a variety of ways to jump?
* To what extent can students keep the rhythm by matching one jump to each drumbeat?
* Can children do all the different jumps in sequence?

MATH

Bodies in Motion

Learning About Shapes

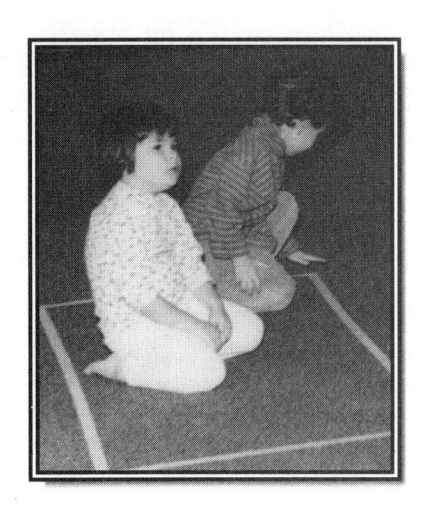

In this activity, children explore all the components of shapes with a partner and on their own. By making shapes with their bodies, they learn how their muscles and bones work together to create angles and curves as well as how to recognize shapes around them.

Materials

- drawings of basic shapes (circle, square, triangle, rectangle, spiral)
- masking tape
- paper and pencil
- two paper bags
- taped music or drum

Warm-Up

Begin by explaining that shapes are everywhere around us, including parts of our own bodies. Tell children they will do movements to

MATH

recognize these shapes. Hold up two contrasting shapes, one angular (a square or triangle) and one curved (a circle or oval). Ask children to describe the shapes and their qualities. They might say they see something round or pointy. Help them build vocabulary by introducing words for the shapes, such as angular, curved, sharp, or smooth. List these descriptive words under a drawing of each shape. Ask children if they can show a partner how some parts of their body can make an angular or curved shape. Call on a few students to share such shapes with the group.

Creative Movement

1 Have students stand in a circle, each an arm's length apart. Put on music and lead them in a brief warm-up of angular and curving motions. First, bend each arm at right angles, then bend both knees and freeze this pointy shape. Now repeat the same sequence using curved arms and slightly bent knees for contrast. Have children use their arms, legs, wrists, and waist to show the following shapes: triangle, circle, and square. Next, ask them to choose a partner to make two-person triangles, circles, and squares. Ask some students to demonstrate to the group the shapes they made alone and then with their partners. Comment on how each body part helps to make a shape: "Look how Jim bends his elbows and knees to make a square." A partner shape for a triangle might have two children pressing against each other's hands while leaning in toward each other.

2 Make masking tape squares, circles, ovals, and triangles on the floor, and assign three or four children to each shape. Ask them to lie down and arrange themselves along the lines of the shape, covering all

81

MATH

the sides, curves, and/or angles. To help them get a better sense of the shape, ask children to walk, then hop or slide along the edges of their shape. Be sure each group gets to visit all the other tape shapes.

3 Here's how to play a game of "shapes in motion": Put several folded pieces of paper, each with a drawing and the name of the shape (circle, triangle, oval), in one bag; in another bag, put pieces of paper with action words written on them (hop, spin, wiggle). Ask a student to choose a piece of paper from each bag and call out the words for the others to act out: "Freeze a circle shape, then make it hop in place." Use a music cue or drum signal for starting and stopping. Include several combinations of shapes and movements.

MATH

Resources

BOOKS

Beach Creatures by Michael K. Smith. Steck-Vaughn, 1997.

Dancing Echoes for the Eye: Poems to Celebrate Patterns in Nature by Barbara Juster Esbensen. HarperCollins, 1996.

Shapes, Shapes, Shapes by Tana Hoban. Greenwillow, 1986.

So Many Circles, So Many Squares by Tana Hoban. HarperCollins, 1998.

MUSIC

Pieces of Africa. Kronos Quartet. Wea/Atlantic/Nonesuch.

Extending the Lesson

Go on a shape scavenger hunt in the classroom and later, perhaps, around the school or neighborhood. Ask children to look around for shapes and describe them. Possibilities might include rectangles in the windows, circles in the lights, and squares on the linoleum floor. Have children stand near the shape they see and make the shape with their body. Have the others guess the shape and the object it is meant to imitate. Outdoors, children might find oval shapes in leaves, cylinders in tree trunks, or squares in the sidewalk.

After the scavenger hunt, discuss all the places children found circles, squares, triangles, and other shapes. Chart the results, and keep adding to the list as you conduct scavenger hunts in new places.

Assessment Checklist

Children who make the connection between visual observation and physical replication develop both cognitive and physical competence. Things to look for include:

* Can children use their body parts to create both angular and curved shapes?
* Can children identify shapes around them and recreate the shapes with their bodies?
* To what extent can a student work with a partner to create shapes?

MATH

Design a Dance

Inventing Patterns

Children explore an important math concept by making patterns with their own bodies and in the process have fun creating a dance.

Materials

- taped music or drum
- colored plastic hoops (see Resources, page 20) or large, colored construction paper cut into large shapes (basic red, yellow, blue, and green work best)

Warm-Up

Ask students about patterns: "What makes a pattern a pattern? How do you know what comes next in a pattern? Can you give an example of a pattern?" (Answers may include something that repeats, clapping rhythms or beads arranged in a repeating color sequence.) Then ask children to think about different kinds of movements; for instance, jumps, spins, or hops. Invite volunteers to demonstrate two or three movements they can link together and repeat. Tell them they will use some of these movements to put together a dance.

MATH

Creative Movement

1. On a cleared space on the floor, lay out in a straight line a repeating color pattern using the hoops or the shapes. Ask students to describe the pattern they notice (red, yellow, blue, green, red, yellow, blue, green . . .).

2. Now have children put together a dance pattern. First, tell them that in the red hoop (or shape) they can do four lively hops. Then turn them into choreographers by asking them to suggest motions for the yellow hoop, then for the blue hoop, and then the green (for instance, spin, wiggle, stomp, respectively). Clap your hands (or hit the drum), counting one-two-three-four for each movement in each hoop. Have one child complete the entire sequence before allowing the next one to begin.

3. After everyone has practiced the four motions, put down four four more hoops so that the entire dance sequence can be repeated. Now get the whole class dancing: Ask children to do the

MATH

Resources

BOOKS
Design a Dance by Susan Kuklin. Hyperion, 1998.

MUSIC
Yearning and Harmony. Tri Atma with Klaus Netzle. Fortuna Records.

four motions, jumping immediately from one hoop to the next when you finish counting to four so that the children behind them can begin the sequence. One after another, children become part of a pattern dance in which color is the cue for a motion.

4 Keep the drumbeat constant, and talk students through the dance: "Hop two-three-four, spin two-three-four, run in place two-three-four, wiggle two-three-four." Counting and naming movements help cement the ideas and the sequence for children. Have half the group watch the other half dance to get a better sense of what a movement pattern looks like.

Extending the Lesson

Encourage children to design their own dances. For instance, they can invent mood or nature dances by matching colors with emotions or natural elements. They might use red for angry gestures, yellow for happy ones. Blue might inspire swimming motions through the "ocean"; green might suggest the branches of a tree swaying in the wind. Incorporate children's "recipes" to build a classroom collection of dances to practice.

Assessment Checklist

Using imagery generates many movement ideas to associate with color patterns. Once movements are put into these patterns, children learn the sequence based on the colors. Coordinating all this takes a lot of concentration. Here's what to look for:

* What ideas do children use to create movements for the patterns?
* To what extent can students replicate the pattern of steps each time?
* Can children maintain the beat while dancing the pattern steps?

MATH

Parachute Games
Exploring One-to-One Correspondence

When children play a matching game with a parachute's colors, they learn about one-to-one correspondence in an engaging and direct way.

Materials

* taped music
* multicolored parachute (see Resources, page 91)

Tip

To make your own parachute, cut four different-colored twin sheets in half diagonally, then sew them together as two sets of alternating color triangles—for example, red, yellow, blue, and green, then the same sequence again. Cut a four-inch hole in the middle for air to escape. Optional: Round the corners to make a circle. Make a 1/4-inch hem.

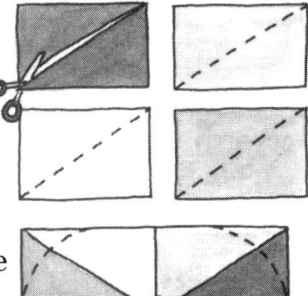

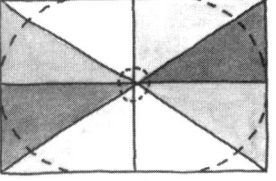

MATH

Warm-Up

Tell children that they will play a gigantic matching game with their bodies and a play parachute. Ask them to name the colors of the parachute. Explain that in the game, they will match themselves to one color. Add that when all the colors (children) are working together, the parachute will move properly.

Creative Movement

1 Stand in the center of a large circle of seated children, and demonstrate how they are to hold on to the parachute material with both hands. Emphasize that the parachute game works best when everyone moves together at the same time. Then spread out the parachute material onto their laps.

2 With everyone holding on to the parachute, have children stand up and create a "classroom thunderstorm." Start with little shakes for the inital drops of rain, then more energetic shakes as the storm builds, finally jumping and shaking to indicate thunder

MATH

and lightning. Reverse the process and stop when the rain stops. Ask everyone to sit down with the empty parachute "cloud" in their laps.

3 Have each child hold on to a color panel with both hands. Tell a brief story about how the parachute can become an "ocean" in which all colors of fish swim and roll in the waves. Practice making the ocean by asking children holding a green section to send a "wave" by lifting and shaking the parachute so the motion is received by the person sitting directly opposite. Repeat using all the colors.

4 Then tell children they will take turns swimming in the ocean according to what color fish they are. First, establish rules about how the fish can swim safely: Swimmers must crawl on and off the parachute to avoid slipping; they must lie down to swim and roll; and they must be careful not to bump other fish. Now explain that the fish will swim and roll over in the ocean waves and then swim (crawl) back to their "home color." Start by calling on the red fish to take their turn. Have other children shake the parachute to

MATH

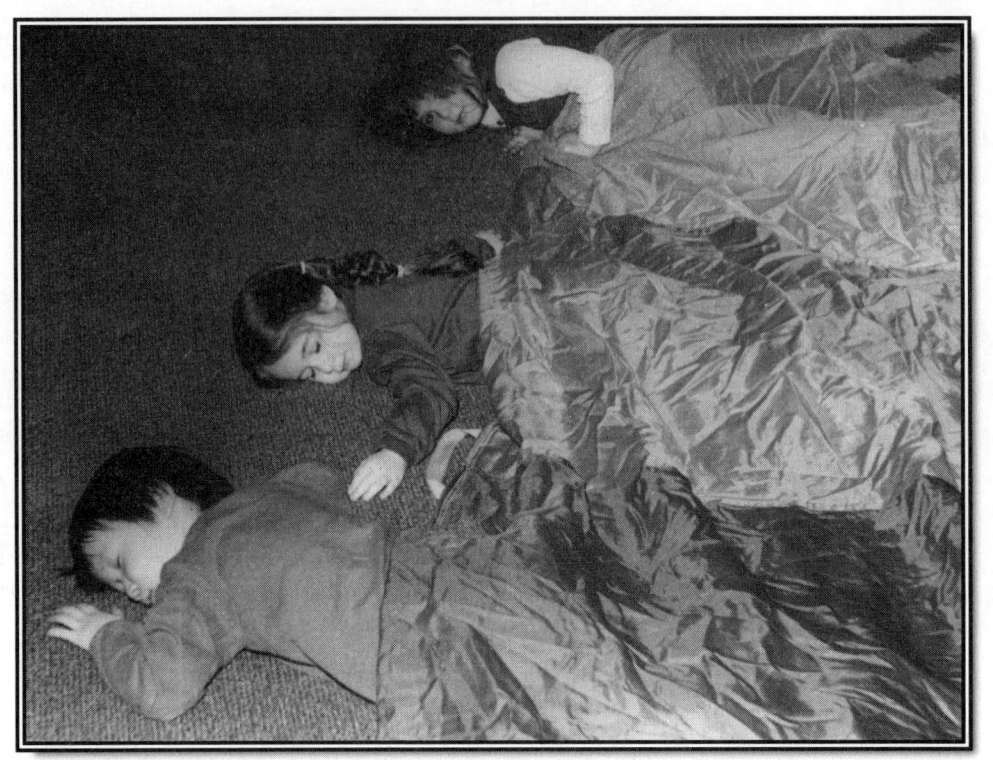

make the ocean waves. Play some flowing music, stopping it when you want the red fish to return to their home color. Let each color group have a turn.

5 End this lesson by having children in each color section lie down in turn, holding the material of the parachute under their chins like a giant blanket. Then tell them to find a favorite resting position, close their eyes, and breathe in through the nose and out through the mouth three times. Conduct a smooth transition by having children in each color group in turn walk to the next place (a line, the meeting area, their desks, and so on).

Extending the Lesson

Tell children they will work together to put up a colorful circus tent. Demonstrate the process for them with these hand motions:

1. Raise your hands above your head.
2. Pull the parachute down behind your back.
3. Sit down on the material.

MATH

Resources

BOOKS
Swimmer by Shelley Gill. Paws IV Publishing, 1995.

Swimmy by Leo Lionni. Pantheon, 1963.

EQUIPMENT
Parachutes. Sportime: 800-283-5700 www.sportime.com

Now ask children to hold on to their section of the parachute material. Tell them that when you count to three, they should all lift up the parachute, pull it behind their backs, and sit down on it. The entire group will then be sitting inside a tent, which should stay up for about a minute and a half.

Tip

A play parachute, whether purchased or homemade, can be enjoyed by all ages. Invite parents, grandparents, and friends to join you and children for an end-of-year picnic, and bring the parachute!

Assessment Checklist

The parachute fosters teamwork as children quickly learn the activities will only succeed if they all cooperate. Each activity also requires children to follow a prescribed sequence. Here's what to look for:

* To what extent can children follow all the instructions for carrying out the activities?
* Can children coordinate their movements with the rest of the group?
* Can children match their actions to their color when it is called?

SCIENCE

Falling Leaves

Exploring Seasonal Changes

Watching leaves fall and playing with them is one of autumn's joys. In this activity, children explore nature's cycles as they re-create the path of a leaf.

Materials

- taped music with a slow, floating quality (see Resources, page 94) or drum
- real or construction paper autumn leaves
- photograph or picture of an autumn tree

Warm-Up

Talk with children about how autumn affects the leaves in the trees—how they change colors and then fall. Suggest that they mimic the ways a leaf twists and floats as it falls. Invite a few students to demonstrate some of these motions with their hands; for instance, reaching up high and slowly swaying down using both hands as if they were floating to the floor.

SCIENCE

Creative Movement

1 Create a "woods in autumn" atmosphere by bringing in colorful leaves (or cutting them out of paper). Hold each one up, then let it drop while children brainstorm words to describe its path: *rocks* back and forth, *floats, spins, tumbles, twirls*. Chart these words and suggest a few that have not been mentioned: *sway, swirl,* and *drift*, for instance.

2 Ask children to lift up their hands and copy the path of a floating, tumbling, twirling leaf. Then choose a space for them to re-create the path of a leaf with their bodies. Indicate the path by posting or drawing a picture of a tree at one end of the room and placing a leaf (for the leaf pile) at the other end.

3 Group students at the "tree" end of the room. Tell them that in their roles as falling leaves they should start with their hands reaching up high into the tree branches to indicate they are still attached to the tree, and then spin, sway, and float all the way to the designated leaf pile. Suggest that they start on tiptoe and gradually get lower and lower, crouching as they drift and twirl, until they are gently rolling along the floor toward the leaf pile.

4 Put on the music and send the leaves on their way, one by one, with a tap for each. When all children have reached the leaf pile, ask them to relax and listen to the music. Repeat the game, tapping each resting leaf when it's time to walk slowly back to the tree area and attach to the branches to begin again.

SCIENCE

Resources

BOOKS
Autumn Leaves by Ken Robbins. Scholastic, 1998.

Why Do Leaves Change Color? by Betsy Maestro. HarperCollins, 1994.

MUSIC
Adagio molto, "The Autumn," *The Four Seasons*. Antonio Vivaldi. Musical Heritage Society, Inc.

Canon in D. Pachelbel. London: Weekend Classics.

Extending the Lesson

Children also learn by watching each other. Have half the group watch the other half travel the leaf pathway. Add interest by asking the leaves to freeze their positions. Then ask the audience to notice and comment on the leaf shapes and locations in their fall. Switch groups and repeat. Encourage students to try out any new movements they observed.

Assessment Checklist

Creative movement such as imitating falling leaves helps children make connections between the world around them and their imagination, and stimulates their expressive capacity. Here's what to watch for:

✹ Can children re-create the twisting, turning, swirling path of the leaf?

✹ To what extent can students express their observations through movement qualities such as floating, swaying, and other smooth, slow motions?

✹ Do children expand their vocabulary in describing the falling leaves?

SCIENCE

Snowflakes and Icicles

Freezing and Thawing

Children swirl around the room, freeze into a shape, and then melt to enact part of the water cycle. They also build their vocabulary by learning to generate contrasting frozen (sharp) shapes with fluid (melting) ones.

Materials

- taped music or drum
- snowflake cutout (see directions, below)

Optional:
- *The Snowy Day* (see Resources, page 98)
- frozen popsicle and dish for it to melt in

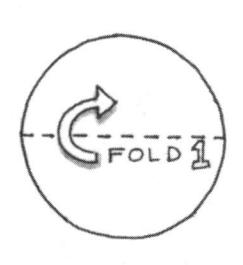

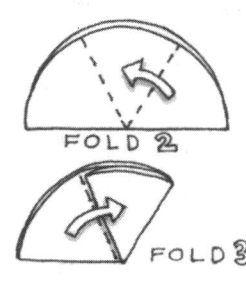

95

SCIENCE

Warm-Up

Ask children what they know about snowflakes—their shape, what they're made of, and how they change when it gets warmer. (If you choose, read them *The Snowy Day*.) Discuss what happens when snow or ice melts. Where does it go? How do snowflakes or icicles change shape when they melt? Ask a student to freeze into a tall icicle or sharp snowflake shape and then slowly melt into a spread-out puddle shape on the floor while you count to 10. Ask children to describe how a body moves as it changes from an icicle to a puddle shape. How are muscles used differently in these shapes? Children might respond that their bodies are stiff, then very loose or limp. Chart as many words as possible to describe the shapes and what happens to them in the freezing and melting processes.

Creative Movement

1. Using the snowflake cutout pattern, ask children to tell you what they notice about the snowflake's shape. Point out the snowflake's sharp angles. Invite children to experiment with finding all the parts of their body that can make pointy shapes, such as their elbows, knees, wrists, and waist. Ask for demonstrations others can copy. Turn on the music or bang the drum, and ask children to create and hold a sharp shape to the count of 10, then make a different one when you call out, "Change!" Tell children to look around and get ideas from all the different shapes they see.

2. Add to students' enjoyment and develop their skill in holding a position by having them add motion to their shape. For instance, invite them to assume their favorite sharp snowflake shape and hop around the room, spin in place, or wiggle. Wiggles soon turn into giggles as children realize how much fun it is to add variety to movement. Count to 10 and call out, "Change shapes!" Then ask them to spin, wiggle, hop, or jump their shapes around the room.

3. Hold up your paper snowflake again and ask children to watch its swirling, twirling motion as it drifts to the floor. Tell them they too will swirl and twirl around the room holding their

SCIENCE

favorite snowflake shape without bumping into other flakes. Put on the music and have them swirl until it stops, at which point they can change to a new shape. Repeat this exercise three or four times.

4 Tell children it is getting much colder and they are turning into icicles—tall, stiffly frozen shapes. As you count or beat the drum to 10, the icicles slowly melt down and spread out into a puddle on the floor. Ask them to notice how their bodies feel as they change from stiff to loose.

5 Put all the elements together: Invite children to take a snowflake shape and swirl it around the room. When the music or drum stops, they change into icicles and melt down to the floor. Then ask them to swirl as snowflakes again and, when the music stops, attach to one or two other snowflakes and then together turn into icicles. Children learn to adjust and respond to each other as they melt their stuck-together icicle to the ground. End the lesson by tapping students in turn and asking them to swirl their snowflake in slow motion to get on line or go to their seats.

SCIENCE

Resources

BOOKS

All About Snow and Ice by Stephen Krensky. Scholastic, 1994.

Snowflake Bentley by Jacqueline Briggs Martin. Houghton Mifflin, 1998.

Snow Is Falling by Franklyn M. Branley. Crowell, 1986.

Snow on Snow on Snow by Cheryl Chapman. Dial, 1994.

The Snowy Day by Ezra Jack Keats. Puffin Books, 1962.

MUSIC
Largo, "The Winter," *The Four Seasons*. Antonio Vivaldi. Library of the Great Arts.

Extending the Lesson

To develop children's observation and interpretation skills, put a popsicle or ice cubes in a dish by the window to melt. Ask children to draw pictures of what happens at each stage, and tape them up in sequence. In the meeting area, have students describe what they drew while others act it out with the motions they have just been using.

Assessment Checklist

Learning to shape the body to represent frozen and melted water adds to a child's movement skills and expressive capacity. Here's what to look for:

✸ In what different ways can each child change from sharp, stiff shapes to loose, limp shapes?

✸ Are children able to work closely and cooperatively in the "melting" groups?

✸ Can children easily adapt from fast swirling to slow melting?

SCIENCE

Monkey Make-Believe

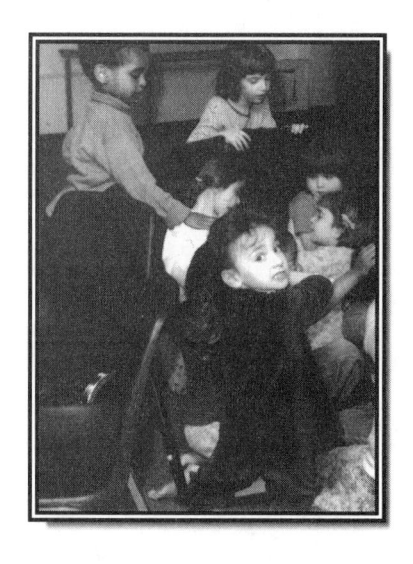

Life in a Rainforest

In this game of cooperative musical chairs, students explore a rainforest monkey's life. They re-create the monkey's movements while learning about its habits and habitat.

Materials

- sturdy chairs (one per three to four students)
- taped music
- large cloth or towel (about 2 by 3 feet, one per student)
- book about monkeys (optional, see Resources, page 102)

Warm-Up

Have a discussion with students about the different sections of the rainforest: the emergent layer, the canopy, the understory, and the forest floor. Then ask them how they think monkeys move through

SCIENCE

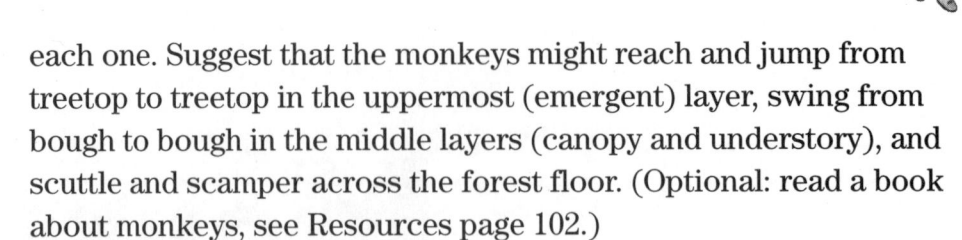

each one. Suggest that the monkeys might reach and jump from treetop to treetop in the uppermost (emergent) layer, swing from bough to bough in the middle layers (canopy and understory), and scuttle and scamper across the forest floor. (Optional: read a book about monkeys, see Resources page 102.)

Once you've brainstormed a list of monkey movements, have students demonstrate some of them. Children might crouch down on all fours and sway from side to side or reach up high and leap about, swinging around the room.

Creative Movement

Create a rainforest by arranging chairs in a circle, the seats facing outward to serve as the monkeys' tree homes. Tell children that when you turn on the music, they will pretend they are rainfor-

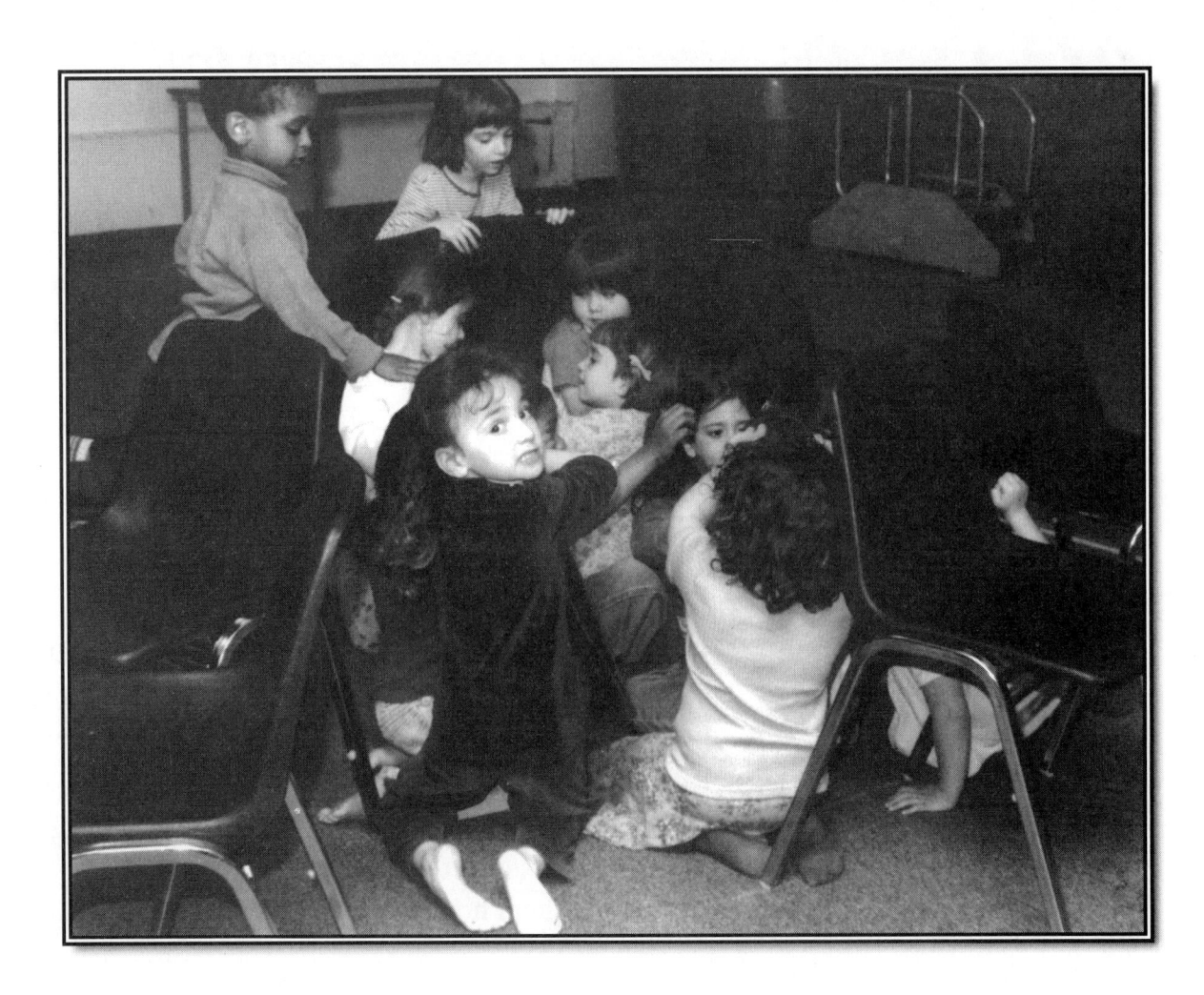

SCIENCE

est monkeys gathering food from all the different layers of the rainforest: top, middle, and bottom. Divide the group into these three layers. Tell children that the monkeys scampering around on the forest floor, or bottom layer, must come out first, then the ones in the middle layer, and finally the ones from the top layer. They might also like to find a monkey friend with whom to play a monkey game of pantomime.

2 Tell children that when you stop the music, they must return "home" gently so as not to bump their monkey friends. They can "groom" each other once they settle into their tree chairs. Then turn on the music.

3 After the monkeys have gathered food and played with each other, stop the music and have children return to their tree homes. Repeat the game several times, but each time the monkeys leave home, act as a "cutter" and remove a chair or two. Challenge the monkeys to work together to find ways of keeping each other safe in their shrinking tree home. They might help hold each other on top of the remaining chairs or squeeze underneath them. On one repetition, invite the monkeys to try different games with different partners. You can stop the activity to have some groups demonstrate their monkey play games. This will give other children ideas to try out.

4 Repeat the game until there is only one chair for every five children left. Children will need to cooperate to fit everyone onto the remaining chairs, hugging each other on top of the chairs and squeezing into tight little balls under the chairs.

5 Gather children into a circle and invite them to describe their reactions to the game. You might ask questions, such as "How did you help each other? How did it feel having to share a small space? Can you imagine how hard it is for real monkeys to live when they don't have enough trees? What kinds of problems might they have, and what can people do to help them?"

SCIENCE

Resources

BOOKS
Monkey by Caroline Arnold. Morrow Junior Books, 1993.

Now I Know Monkeys by Patricia Whitehead. Troll, 1982.

When the Monkeys Come Back by Kristine Franklin. Atheneum, 1994.

MUSIC
Deep Forest. Sony Music: Celine Music/Synsound, 1992.

Extending the Lesson

Now children can create their own monkey family groups, forest homes, and adventures. Give each student a chair and a large piece of cloth to work with. Some may choose to push their chairs together to form family groups, while others may choose to live alone. The way students decide to use their cloths will vary as well, whether as a cover or as a nest. Suggest that students teach a monkey friend a new game or bring a new monkey friend home for a sleepover.

Assessment Checklist

In this activity, mind and body work together in a creative way that lays the foundation for artistic processes. Here are a few things to look for:

* Can children use their bodies expressively when acting roles at all layers?
* Can children translate their ideas and feelings about monkeys into gestures and movement?
* Can students interact with others while staying in character and using monkey gestures to communicate?

SCIENCE

Balancing Buildings

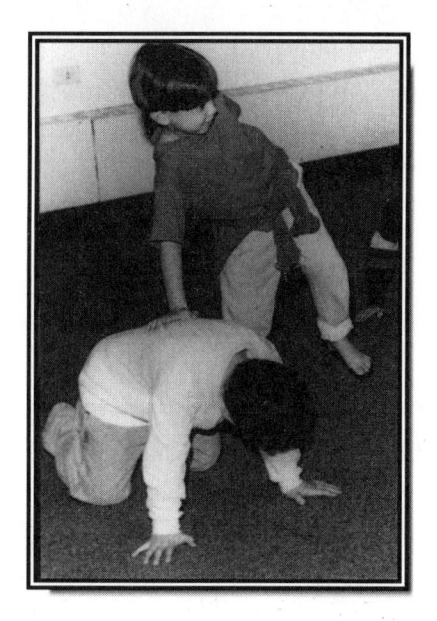

Discovering Gravity

Children can experiment with an unseen force, gravity, as they discover how to sense and use weight as well as how to balance with a partner.

Materials

Optional:
* slow taped music or drum
* *What It Feels Like to Be a Building* (see Resources, page 107)

Warm-Up

Go on a building inspection by taking a walk around the school, your block, the neighborhood, or looking around the classroom and out the window at other buildings. (Optional: Read aloud *What It Feels Like to Be a Building*.)

Ask children to share what they know about how buildings are constructed. Point out that every building has a basic structure of vertical supports, which hold up the building, and horizontal crossbeams, which balance the building sideways so it doesn't topple over.

103

SCIENCE

Have children look around the classroom and guess where the supports and balances are. (Sometimes these are more apparent in the cafeteria or lobby, where you may see actual pillars.) Invite the school custodian in to discuss the building with children, and take them to areas in the building where they can see the supporting structures. Take pictures of these features to copy later on in creative movement activities.

When children construct block buildings, ask them to think about where the supports and balances in their own bodies are and show them to others. Explain that in our own bodies, our bones and muscles support and balance us.

Creative Movement

Begin by having children stand with their eyes closed and feet apart. Ask them to try and sense where their weight is by leaning slightly forward, returning to center, then leaning slightly back. (Make sure the leaning is subtle enough so that no one loses his or her balance and falls down.)

104

SCIENCE

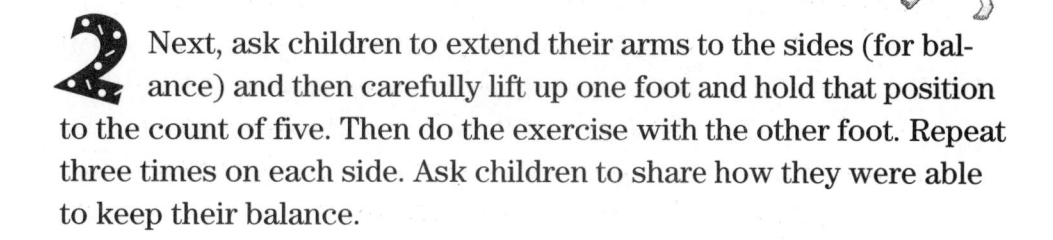

2 Next, ask children to extend their arms to the sides (for balance) and then carefully lift up one foot and hold that position to the count of five. Then do the exercise with the other foot. Repeat three times on each side. Ask children to share how they were able to keep their balance.

3 Now have children work with partners to experiment with making supports and balances using their own bodies. Explain that one partner will be the support while the other will balance on him or her. (Later, they will switch.) Instruct the support children to take strong positions they can hold without toppling, feet wide apart or in a bridge shape on hands and feet.

4 Put on slow, flowing music or beat steadily on the drum as the partners construct their "body buildings." Ask the balancing partners to slowly and carefully rest their weight in an interesting shape (which they must hold, frozen) on the supporting partners. For instance, a balancer might place a hand on the supporter's

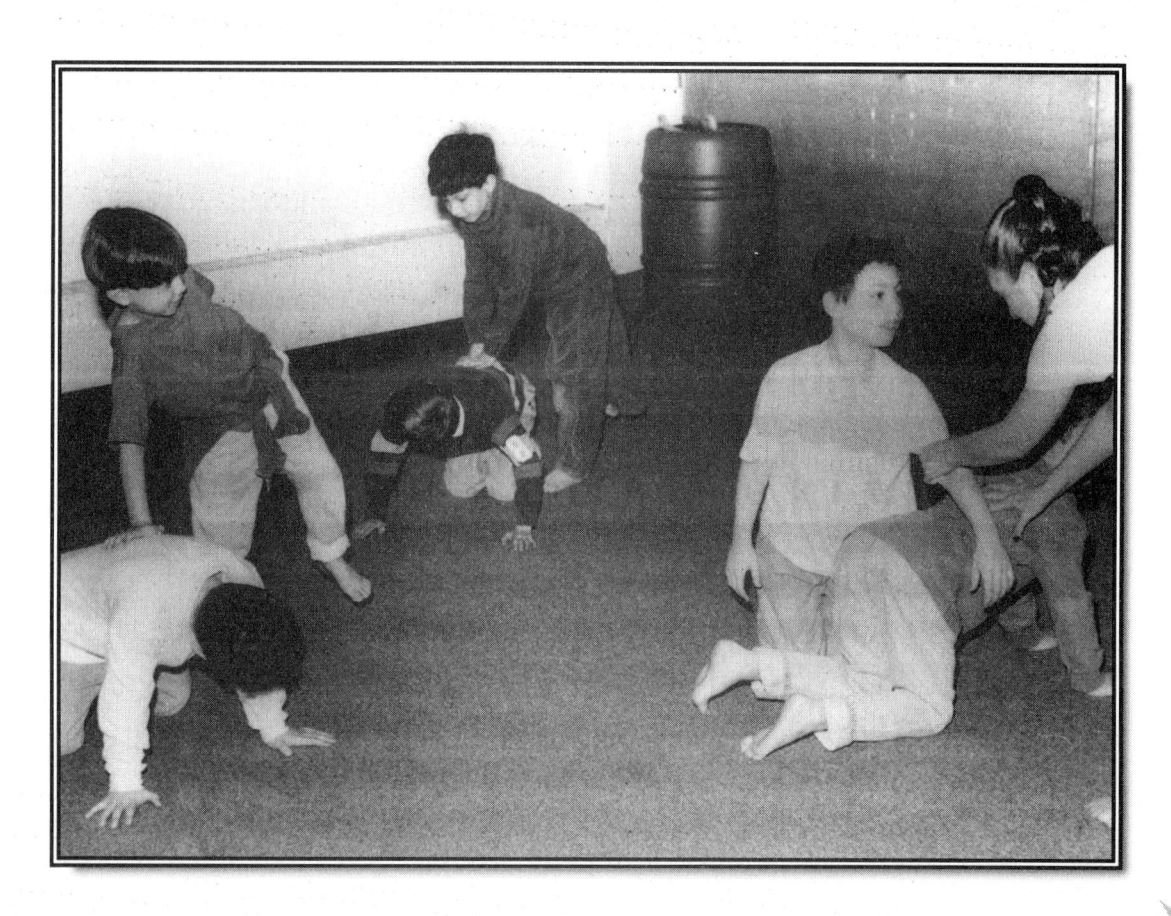

SCIENCE

shoulders while holding up one leg and one arm. Have everyone freeze and take a quick look at all the buildings. Ask one or two of the best buildings to demonstrate their balancing shapes. Then have the partners switch roles and repeat the exercise.

5 Once everyone has had a turn at both roles, start a new exercise. Tell the balancers they will learn more about balancing by carrying their own weight after their partners slowly move out from supporting them. Give the balancers time to prepare by counting to five before the supporters remove themselves. Then have partners switch roles and repeat.

6 Conclude the lesson by asking children to share strategies they used to construct and keep their shapes steady. They might say, "I had all my weight on the standing leg" or "I listened to the count and got ready on two." Ask what problems they had and how they solved them. Then ask what kinds of problems they think builders have in trying to construct strong, safe buildings. Make a two-column chart to compare and contrast their responses.

Extending the Lesson

Now include everyone in a group building. Tell children that each of them will add to the building by attaching to another person, freezing their shape and keeping steady enough so that someone else can attach to them. (Be sure to tell children they must attach to each other gently.)

★ Have children assume a variety of shapes, some high, some low, so that the building looks interesting. Start by having one child get down on his or her hands and knees to be the first support. Tap students one by one to signal their turn to add themselves to the building.

★ Comment on the developing form: "I see children building high, pointy shapes with some low, curved ones attached. Who can make another kind of balancing shape?"

★ Add some extra excitement. Challenge children to find their own balance and hold it as you signal a few children with a tap to carefully crawl out of their positions, seeing if the remaining children can still hold their shapes!

SCIENCE

Resources

BOOKS

Amazing Buildings by Philip Wilkinson. Dorling Kindersley, 1993.

Architecture Shapes, *Architecture Counts*, and *Architecture Colors* (three books) by Michael J. Crosbie and Steve Rosentha. Preservation Press, 1993.

What It Feels Like to Be a Building by Forrest Wilson. Preservation Press, 1988.

MUSIC
"I Live in the City," *Artichokes*. Malvina Reynolds.

Hush. Yo Yo Ma and Bobby McFerrin. Sony Masterworks.

Assessment Checklist

Throughout this lesson, children use both mind and body to interpret what they learn about buildings and gravity. Here are some things to notice:

✺ Are children able to alternate roles as support and balance?

✺ To what extent can children acting as balances serve as their own supports once the support partners remove themselves?

✺ Can individual children invent a variety of balanced shapes? Can they work in partnership to create successful buildings?

SCIENCE

A Spaghetti Feast

Changes in Properties

Children learn how cooking causes changes in the properties of a familiar food in this cooperative game that has them prepare an imaginary spaghetti supper.

Materials

- sheet or other large piece of fabric (see Resources, page 111)
- lively taped music or drum
- *Pasta Please* (optional, see Resources)

Warm-Up

Ask students what happens when you cook spaghetti. What cooking steps are used? What are the specific qualities of cooked and uncooked spaghetti? What changes happen to spaghetti as it is cooked? Then pantomime the entire process step by step so students can reenact it later. Start by filling a pot with water, then

SCIENCE

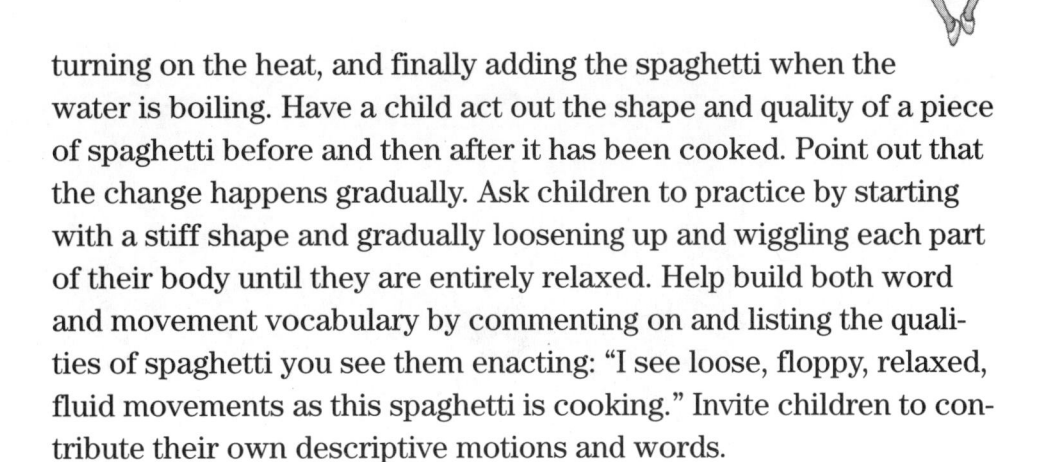

turning on the heat, and finally adding the spaghetti when the water is boiling. Have a child act out the shape and quality of a piece of spaghetti before and then after it has been cooked. Point out that the change happens gradually. Ask children to practice by starting with a stiff shape and gradually loosening up and wiggling each part of their body until they are entirely relaxed. Help build both word and movement vocabulary by commenting on and listing the qualities of spaghetti you see them enacting: "I see loose, floppy, relaxed, fluid movements as this spaghetti is cooking." Invite children to contribute their own descriptive motions and words.

Creative Movement

1 Divide the group into "cooks" and "spaghetti." (Later on, have them switch roles.)

2 Choose a spot in the room for the cooking pot and another spot to designate the box where the spaghetti will wait for the cooks. Have the cooks begin by filling the imaginary pot with water

109

SCIENCE

and salt, then turning on the heat and waiting for the water to boil. In the meantime, the spaghetti children line up stiffly in their box and wait for the cooks to come and get them.

3 When the water is boiling, play music (or beat the drum) as each cook takes a spaghetti child by the hand to the pot. Once the cook's spaghetti is in, the cook begins stirring the water. When all the spaghetti has been put in, the cooks will be standing around outside the pot stirring while the spaghettis bob stiffly up and down, swirling around in response to the cooks' stirring, and gradually getting looser and more wiggly. Children may even lie on the floor with their arms and legs wiggling in the air.

4 When the cooks count to three and pour out the water, the spaghetti lie limp and still. The cooks bring the large piece of material (red chiffon makes a great "tomato sauce") to cover the cooked spaghetti and sit around to have a pretend taste. Make a smooth transition by asking the spaghettis to walk quietly to a designated space while the cooks slowly remove the sauce. Then the cooks and the spaghetti switch roles.

SCIENCE

Resources

BOOKS
More Spaghetti, I Say by Rita Golden Gelman. Scholastic, 1977.

Pasta Please by Melvin Berger. Newbridge Educational Publications, 1997.

Strega Nona: An Old Tale by Tomie De Paola. Prentice-Hall, 1975.

MUSIC
Italian Capriccio, Op. 45. Peter Tchaikovsky.

EQUIPMENT
Lightweight nylon fabric: 9 by 9 feet. Canopies of Color. Chime Time: 800-477-5057; www.chimetime.com

5 Later on, invite children to describe their reactions, either in writing or aloud. Some questions to ask include, "What was your favorite part about being the spaghetti? How can you move in the pot without bumping other spaghetti? What would you like to add to this game?"

Extending the Lesson

Read aloud the book *Pasta Please*. It recounts, through lively photographs, how pasta gets to the table, starting with the planting and harvesting of the wheat, the mixing of raw ingredients that make the spaghetti (wheat, eggs, oil, and water), and finally the cooking. As you read, groups of children can act out each sequence. You might like to invite a parent in to cook a favorite pasta recipe from scratch with children. Many cultures around the world use pasta or noodles in their dishes.

Assessment Checklist

In this exercise, children must remember and perform a sequence of events as well as interpret changing and contrasting qualities. Here's what to look for:

* Are students able to show contrasting qualities of stiffness and looseness in their movements?
* Can students easily re-create the sequence of events necessary to cook the pasta?

Notes